The Anxious Attachment Handbook

A Practical Guide to Heal Your Anxious Attachment and Improve Your Relationship

ROMI SIEGEL

This book is dedicated to all the beautiful people healing from their anxious attachment. You are all superstars!

Also, to my parents, who managed to mess me up sufficiently, so I have enough material for the book.

ACKNOWLEDGMENTS

I'm eternally grateful to the amazing Anxiously Coupled community, who provided me with lots of encouragement and insight into their attachment style and relationship struggles, and to my beautiful friends, who have been my support system in my turbulent adult years. It's been a real journey growing up with you guys!

CONTENTS

About attachment styles

1
Attachment theory

Humans have powerful survival instincts from birth. One of the strongest is a baby's need to survive and rely on an adult for safety and nurturing. Babies naturally desire to ensure that their basic needs are met by a parent, caregiver, or other significant person in their lives. **Depending on their emotional environment and the type of care available, children develop different strategies for achieving this. The study of this primitive instinct is known as attachment theory.** Attachment theory was methodized by psychiatrist and psychoanalyst John Bowlby. Then in the 1960s and 70s, developmental psychologist Mary Ainsworth introduced the concept of secure attachment and developed the theory of several attachment patterns in infants.

Researchers discovered that one of the most important elements in the formation of attachment is attunement. Essentially, attunement means being in tune with others, being aware of and being responsive to them. Emotional attunement entails being in tune with oneself first, then with others, and finally with one's environment. An adult can help the child establish a secure attachment by responding to their needs. This establishes a foundation for the child to explore the world. On the other hand, a parent's or primary caregiver's lack of attunement or misattunement results in the child developing an insecure attachment. This book explores the insecure attachment style called anxious attachment, discovering how it develops, how it resurfaces in our adult relationships, and how we can unlearn and replace it with secure attachment practices.

2
Attachment healing

Being anxiously attached is neither our choice nor our fault, however working towards earned secure attachment will have a significant impact on the health of our relationships. To develop a more secure connection and a healthier relationship with others, we must learn about our attachment style and adopt the tools to help us cultivate a healthy connection. There is a widespread belief that attachment styles – formed in childhood – stay with us for the rest of our lives. However, our attachment style evolves as we develop and change through life. It can also take a conscious decision to rewire how we conduct our relationships, and that's where attachment healing comes into the picture. **Anxious attachment healing happens through developing self-awareness, self-regulation, and correcting our emotional responses to triggering stimuli.** This involves recognizing and acknowledging the pain of the experience and replacing it with something positive. Essentially, it means noticing our anxiously attached patterns and updating them with positive past or present experiences to rewrite the negative thought pattern that follows. With attachment healing, we can rewire our thoughts and react to our triggers more securely if we stay consistent with the work. In the following chapters, we will discover how to notice our triggers and rewire our thinking, tuning into securely attached best practices.

3
What is an attachment style?

According to attachment theory, the relationship with our parent figure or primary caregiver is the foundation of all relationship dynamics in adulthood. **Attachment styles are used to identify how we relate to others in our life, form relationships, manage conflict and cope on an interpersonal basis.** Attachment styles happen on a spectrum, so we all exhibit our attachment traits to varying degrees.

Our attachment style develops in early childhood, based on the relationships with our primary caregiver. Children have basic needs to be met, such as; soothing, emotional support, love, care, etc. When we are in tune with our primary caregiver, who can meet our needs, we will likely develop a secure attachment style. If we don't meet our needs, then an insecure attachment forms. There are three types of insecure attachments, anxious-preoccupied, dismissive-avoidant, and fearful-avoidant, also referred to as disorganized.

	View of self	Anxiety/ Avoidance
Secure attachment	Positive view of self as well as others	Low anxiety Low avoidance
Anxious attachment	Negative view of self, positive view of others	High anxiety Low avoidance
Avoidant attachment	Positive view of self, negative view of others	Low anxiety High avoidance
Disorganized attachment	Negative view of self, negative view of others	High anxiety High avoidance

4
What is attachment trauma?

Trauma is our emotional, mental, and bodily response to a distressful event that impacts our nervous system, preventing it from functioning normally. It causes feelings of helplessness and reduces our ability to feel our emotions and experiences to the fullest due to an intense emotional shutdown. Traumatic situations can vary significantly from person to person, and it's important to remember that with trauma, its response is more important to consider than its trigger.

Attachment trauma is the disrupted bonding pattern between a child and their primary caregiver. In the case of an insecure attachment, a traumatic event can simply be the lack of parental attunement, like not responding to the child's distress immediately. This trauma moves on a spectrum from abuse or neglect to less obvious behaviors like lack of consistent affection or inconsistent response to the child's needs. One of the earliest forms of relational trauma is attachment trauma, and that's why it plays such an important role in our adult partnership.

5
What is an anxious attachment?

Attachment is how we relate to our partners, based on how we learned to give and receive love when we were children. **Anxious, preoccupied, or ambivalent attachment relationships are impacted by a concern that our need for intimacy, love, and affection will not be reciprocated by our significant other.** People with an anxious attachment style are concerned with the emotional availability of their partner or others close to them, such as friends or family members. Anxious attachers need closeness and intimacy but question whether their partners will meet their emotional needs. Autonomy and independence can make them feel insecure. In addition, they can become distressed if they experience inconsistency or a behavioral pattern change from their partner. Their main concern in a relationship is their fear of rejection and abandonment, which has a profoundly negative impact on their decision-making and how they relate to conflict and problem-solving in the partnership.

6
The different attachment styles

Attachment theory recognizes four different attachment styles; secure, avoidant, anxious, and disorganized, and now that we have gone through what an anxious attachment is, I think it's time to get familiar with the other three, so we have a better picture of attachment theory as a whole.

Secure attachment is the most common in Western society, with approximately over 50% of the US population securely attached. These people experienced a safe and caring relationship with their parents, where the caregiver was attuned to their needs. They developed a positive view of themselves as well as others.

They feel good and content on their own as well as in a relationship, they do not need constant reassurance or soothing, and they don't feel the need to doubt their loved ones. They can give and receive affection in their relationship without attaching a negative meaning to it or overthinking it.

Secure attachment is vital in forming healthy and interdependent adult relationships. Securely attached people are more likely to form confident and healthy relationships with others and maintain a healthy balance of relying on their partner and meeting their own needs. They are open to being vulnerable in their relationships, don't shy away from problem-solving, and show integrity despite hardships.

Securely attached people:

> ➤ Are selfless, generous, and trusting with their partner
> ➤ Can ask for help when needed, can give help when asked
> ➤ Are confident and decisive in their partnerships and life, in general
> ➤ Assume that others have positive intentions

- ➢ Enjoy a healthy balance of time spent alone and others
- ➢ Have a strong sense of personal values
- ➢ Are able to set and respect boundaries
- ➢ Can trust others and themselves
- ➢ Initiate repair and accepts repair attempts

One of the insecure attachment styles is avoidant attachment. Avoidantly attached people tend to dissociate from close relationships and can often come across emotionally distant. This attachment style is independent, self-sufficient, and often uncomfortable relying on others or opening up vulnerably.

People with an avoidant attachment style may have been raised by parents who are strict, emotionally distant, or do not tolerate the expression of feelings. In return, their children tend to become highly independent, withdrawn, and emotionally shut down.

The avoidant adult remains on the surface regarding social or relational interactions. They do not allow deep feelings and, therefore, often have issues with forming a secure and emotionally connected partnership. Avoidant adults often come off as confident high achievers who do well in their careers. But things can be quite challenging when it comes to their love lives. They have difficulty opening up in relationships or letting their partner in. Instead, they keep them at arm's length and often give mixed signals.

Avoidantly attached people:

- ➢ Tend to keep a distance from others, pushing them away when they get too close
- ➢ Lack emotional closeness in relationships, fear intimacy
- ➢ Have difficulties trusting others and opening up or expressing their emotions
- ➢ Are unlikely to seek help in stressful situations
- ➢ Seem distant, unloving, or giving mixed messages

- Are self-reliant, and often isolate themselves
- Are confident in their ability to deal with problems alone
- Are dismissive towards threatening events
- Suppress outward displays of emotions

Disorganised attachment style is the most rare of the insecure attachments. It is often present in people who were physically, verbally, or mentally abused as children. For disorganized adults, perceived fear takes center stage in their lives.

Adults with this attachment style lack a coherent approach to their adult relationships. They deeply crave to be close to their partner; on the other hand, they are too scared to let anyone in. They are disinclined to believe that love and support are available to them because they don't think they deserve it. Disorganized people see rejection, disappointment, and hurt as inevitable parts of a romantic relationship.

Fearful-avoidant attachment develops when a parent fails to respond to their child's distress or feelings of fear. For example, a child might react negatively to a new situation or person. Instead of soothing or reassuring the child, the parent might use punishment or intimidation to stop the child's adverse reaction. Or perhaps the caregiver gives the child positive verbal reassurance but fails to physically embrace them, giving them a hug, touch, or kiss.

Disorganized people:

- May show chaotic, unpredictable, or intense relationship patterns and behaviors
- Have extreme fear of rejection, coupled with difficulty connecting to and trusting others
- Show an extreme need for closeness, paired with trying to avoid physical or emotional closeness
- Have a negative self-image and low self-worth

➤ Have deep-rooted shame, depression, or anxiety

➤ Feel unlovable, inadequate, or unworthy

7
How does anxious attachment form?

Anxious attachment develops when a parent or caregiver is inconsistent with their response to a child's emotional needs. This could mean that the caregiver would sometimes be emotionally available to the child while other times, they would be cold and closed off. Children don't fully understand why their parent is giving them inconsistent emotional care and support. Therefore, they grow up fearful that they won't get the emotional support or love needed at any given time and develop coping mechanisms to ensure they stay close to their attachment figures at any cost. It is important to remember that our parents did the best they could for us with the knowledge available to them, at the emotional awareness they had.

Here are a few possible reasons for parent-child misattunement:

➤ The parent is **preoccupied with their problems**, work, or private life and cannot fully devote themselves to the child's needs. They would sometimes be attuned and attentive, other times dismissive.

➤ The parent is **confused about the child's needs** and doesn't have a well-developed parenting style. This is often the case with first-time parents or parents who are insecure about their parenting practices.

➤ The parent **has anxiety or depression** and uses the child to console or soothe themselves. This emotional hunger of the caregiver prevents them from focusing on the child's need for love and connection.

➤ The parent **has an anxious attachment style** and is preoccupied with their own triggers and traumas. This is very often the case with children developing anxious attachment.

They observe their parent's inconsistent behavior and, as a response, develop those same strategies themselves simply because children model their parent figures.

➤ The parent (often a single parent) **has unmet emotional needs and requires the child to fulfill them**. In this instance, the roles are often reversed, and the child becomes the parent. This is called parentification. Parentification happens when a child is regularly expected to provide emotional or practical support to their parent instead of receiving it themselves. This role reversal can disrupt the natural maturing process, causing long-term negative effects on the child's mental health.

➤ The parent **has substance abuse issues** and is less capable of taking care of their child. They're not as involved or can only show up inconsistently.

➤ The parent **believes that letting the child self-soothe will benefit them later in life**. This parenting technique creates a dynamic where the caregiver is occasionally available to soothe the child's distress. The inconsistency creates a dynamic where the child is unsure of what to expect and confused by mixed signals.

➤ The parent **cannot decide on the best parenting practice** and switches between being overly available and not at all. This can make the child confused about their expectations.

Identifying these patterns could be incredibly painful, so process things compassionately and without judgment. Remember, your parent was probably unaware that their actions would have long-term consequences on your emotional well-being, so try to practice empathy.

8
What other reasons play a part?

Research has shown that the quality of the parents' relationship determines their attachment patterns. **In other words, attachment styles can be passed down from one generation to the next, and children can imitate the anxious attachment of their parents.** In addition, research has also found that parents' practices and techniques to raise their children show the attachment patterns they developed in their childhood. People who grow up with an anxious attachment show inconsistent emotional patterns as parents, and their children react to this by forming their own anxious attachment styles.

This happens because we copy our parents' relational patterns and communication styles as part of our learning process. Children model who they are and how they relate to the world around them through their first interactions with their parents or caregivers, and parents shape these interactions knowingly and unknowingly. This way, they consciously or unconsciously predetermine what their child will become. That is why it is vital to learn about our attachment styles and work on becoming secure, so we can stop passing our attachment style down as generational trauma.

9
The mother wound

Mothers mold us emotionally as well as physically, as a child's sense of self is built upon the relationship with their primary caregiver, who is usually our mother. So when a mother is not available to their child emotionally, a so-called 'mother wound' occurs.

A mother wound can form when the mother:

> ➤ Only provided support to take care of the physical needs of the child but did not provide security, care, or love
> ➤ Didn't help the child understand, label and manage their feelings
> ➤ Didn't allow the expression of negative emotions
> ➤ Was very critical of their children

➢ Expected the child to help with her own physical or emotional needs
➢ Had untreated mental problems or substance abuse issues
➢ Had experienced mental or physical abuse that went untreated, and the trauma prevented them from offering love and support to their children

The most common signs of a mother wound are low self-esteem, lack of emotional awareness, inability to self-soothe and the consistent longing for but lack of nurturing relationships. Adults with the mother wound have never learned to trust; therefore, it is difficult for them to form and maintain the positive relationships that they crave. A mother who is emotionally present for their child is able to tune into their child's feelings and label them, helping the child to manage both negative and positive emotions. This teaches the child to process their negative feelings rather than suppress them and helps them develop a way to regulate their emotions and self-soothe in triggering situations.

10
The father wound

The father wound is a term for an absent father. When a father is physically absent, emotionally distant or abusive, negative or overly critical, it can have long-term consequences for the child's development. Parents are the first people we learn to love and form relationships with. If they are not supportive or available in any way, it can severely impact how we form relationships with others in our adult years.

A father wound can form a father:

➢ Who was absent physically or emotionally
➢ Who was abusive physically, verbally, or emotionally
➢ Who was critical or disapproving of actions, choices, or behaviors

➣ Who used punishments, such as withholding love, or affection

Signs of a father wound:

A father wound can create feelings of **low self-esteem**, of not meeting expectations, not being good enough, and being undeserving of love. As children, we can't understand that our parents are people battling their problems, so we internalize their behavior or reactions as our fault. Low self-esteem can show up as

➣ Never pushing harder and not wanting to progress at work
➣ Difficulty opening up and forming authentic connections with others
➣ Difficulty forming long-lasting relationships and friendships

The father wound also impacts our **perception of the self**. If we are overlooked or criticized by our Father, our inner critic (our internal voice) may tell us that we are unworthy of our Father's love and attention. It can teach us that we are not good enough or important because our father didn't want to spend time with us. So we may start to internalize that something is fundamentally wrong with us, that we are flawed, and even in adulthood, this internal voice keeps reminding us of the perceptions we developed as children. When no one ever helps us correct these false perceptions, they can potentially impact our self-worth in relationships, making us develop defensive tactics to keep love in our lives and even influence the way we pick romantic partners, solve conflicts, or connect to others.

A negative view of relationships

A father wound can impact daughters by giving them a negative view of men and women. This can show up by being attracted to men who are neglectful, abusive, emotionally closed off, or challenging to be around. As people with a father wound never had a role model for a 'man,' they developed their own way of understanding and attracting men. This can resurface in negative coping skills, like promiscuity, expressing connection through sexual intimacy, anxiety, isolation, or total avoidance of intimacy. On the other hand, when fathers connect with their daughters in a meaningful way, it has a positive impact on them. Research suggests that women with a positive relationship with their fathers generally feel better about themselves. They show assertiveness without being aggressive; they have more confidence in relationships and with the other sex.

A father wound can similarly impact sons, causing damaging outcomes to them. It can destroy the core of the developing masculine identity, causing men to struggle through life, believing they never measured up to their father, not being quite sure what it is to be a man.

11
Important skills to learn from our parents

As children, we learn many life skills from our parents, and they are vital to managing our mental, physical and emotional health later in life. However, many of us grew up in homes where there wasn't much emphasis on helping children master these skills or practice them. **This is especially true for anxiously attached people, who learned to shift the focus from themselves to a parent or caregiver, to maintain the connection.** This may have prevented them from learning healthy emotional management and regulation, self-love and healthy self-esteem, effective communication skills, and compassion for themselves and others.

An important skill to learn is to be kind and compassionate to ourselves and others. As children, we need to establish a healthy value system and be brave enough to challenge, change and extend this system as we go through life. This includes respecting our own choices, boundaries, opinions, bodies, health, and well-being, as well as those of others. It also includes not forcing our beliefs or choices on others.

We also need to know how and when to let go of habits or situations that do not align with our beliefs or people who do not respect our needs or choices. If we don't learn compassion for ourselves and others in childhood, then we might grow into adults who lack love and respect for themselves as well as others.

Self-belief and self-confidence are skills that parents teach through reinforcing positive and helping to accept negative experiences and emotions. This way, children are encouraged to take risks to better themselves in life and work towards a better outcome, even when facing setbacks. This mentality helps children see new opportunities and enjoy the process of working towards something rather than giving in at the first sign of failure. Learning this in childhood will make us more confident and competent in everything we do. When our parents do not teach us self-belief and self-confidence, they allow us to internalize our mistakes and wallow in our failures.

With anxious attachment, if we weren't taught proper self-belief and self-confidence, we outsource validation and reassurance to those closest to us. We become unsure about our own choices, thoughts, and even decisions, to the point where we constantly seek reassurance, not to mention that we fail to spot our own needs and meet them ourselves.

Learning to manage their emotions is one of the most important things a child can learn. As children, we learn emotional management from our parents, and if we don't see a positive example of it, we will lack this vital skill in adulthood. Parents teach their children to upregulate their positive and downregulate their negative emotions. If this isn't learned in childhood, then it creates emotionally unstable adults who overthink and overreact and cannot self-soothe in emotionally overwhelming situations, going towards high anxiety or high avoidance.

This is a prominent issue in anxious attachment, as most of us did not have a positive example to teach us healthy emotional regulation. We likely grew up with a mix of positive and negative responses and reactions from our caregivers and internalized this as the norm. As a result, we are easy to trigger and difficult to soothe, even in the presence of loving and caring partners who show nothing but support.

The quality of our **communication skills** impacts our private as well as professional lives. However, most parents don't teach their children to communicate effectively and listen actively.

With anxious attachment, we likely picked up a lot of dysfunctional communication strategies, from stonewalling to nitpicking, and we don't always realize how bad they are. However, cultivating healthy communication skills is a huge part of nurturing a healthy relationship.

12
How can generational trauma contribute to forming an anxious attachment?

When we talk about transgenerational, in other words, intergenerational trauma, we refer to trauma that is passed from a person to their children and grandchildren. This often happens when a parent experiences some form of traumatic experience as a child, impacting their parenting style, personality, outlook on life, behavior, and reactions. Generational trauma is not passed down directly from grandparent to parent to child. Instead, each generation receives a filtered or altered version of what the previous generation experienced.

For example, someone who grew up in a household where emotional and physical neglect is the norm may pass this down to the next generation by meeting their children's physical needs but neglecting to pay attention to their emotional needs, showing next to no affection, caring or emotional support.

When emotional wounds are passed down from generation to generation without healing or resolution, it can severely impact how individuals develop emotionally and cope on a personal or interpersonal basis. With anxious attachment, when a caregiver isn't or is only inconsistently available to the child, then the child is forced to create safety and security for themselves. This often means that a role reversal is created to forge a closer connection to the parent, which can have long-term negative impacts on the caregiver-child bond. A child's first point of reference for relating is with their caregivers and close relatives, so it is often inevitable that they learn to form their own anxious attachment as a way to model the parent.

13
Signs of anxious attachment in children

In the 1930s psychoanalyst John Bowlby treated children with emotional and behavioral disorders. His work made him realize that children with mental health issues had a fractured attachment to their mothers, and he started focusing his career on discovering this. Bowlby acknowledged that social, emotional, and cognitive behavioral problems were more present in children who experienced separation from their mothers. He then proposed that infants have a universal need to seek closeness to their caregiver when experiencing distress.

Research suggests that a child who has developed an anxious attachment toward their primary caregiver may seem visibly anxious when separated from them. They may also be hard to console after the caregiver has returned. Certain childhood events may increase the likelihood of developing an anxious attachment, such as early separation from a parent (adoption), troubled childhood, instances of neglect or mistreatment, or caregivers who showed emotional immaturity: ridiculed the child or became annoyed when the child was in distress.

Signs of anxious attachment in children

> ➤ Unconsolable crying if separated from the caregiver
> ➤ Craving closeness to their attachment figure
> ➤ Being less adventurous than other children while exploring their surroundings
> ➤ Showing more general anxiety than other children
> ➤ Shying away from interacting with strangers
> ➤ Problems regulating and controlling negative emotions
> ➤ Displaying more aggressive behavior and poor social interactions with other children

14
Attachment trauma and its impacts

According to research, people with anxious attachment are more likely to get facts wrong about everyday situations, because their minds falsify memories more than other people's. Researchers suggested that anxiously attached people's feelings get mixed up in everyday situations, which may create false memories about what happened or influence the context in which they perceive everyday occurrences. This finding can be a critical factor in understanding how people with anxious attachment remember their childhood and how they interpret their childhood memories at a later age.

We tend to think of trauma as a significant life event that happened to us, an accident, death, or physical or mental abuse. **However, for many people, childhood trauma was instead the lack of something rather than the presence of any of the above.** Growing up with parents who didn't give us a sense of belonging and didn't consider or validate our thoughts or emotions can be a form of trauma. Not receiving validation or physical or emotional support from our caregiver to the point where we have to learn to process our emotions on our own can be a form of trauma. Not having someone who understands or encourages us while growing up can be a form of trauma. Most of these experiences shape who we become as adults and what coping mechanisms we form later in life.

Most of us who grew up with parents providing inconsistent care and attention don't have a lot of negative memories from our childhood. Or at least not ones that relate to parental misattunement. We remember our childhood fondly, have amazing memories that we cherish and think of our parents as loving and caring people who take great care of us. One reason behind this may be that when facing a traumatic event, our brain creates separation between us and the source of the trauma. If this separation cannot be created – because the source of trauma is also the source of safety, aka our parent – then the separation is created within us. This looks like dissociating from the traumatic event, dismissing negative memories, and internalizing certain situations. Internalizing events can happen in many forms, but one of the most prominent, with the most profound impact on our adult lives, is creating core beliefs. A core belief is a deep-rooted belief about ourselves that we create from suppressed emotions and childhood memories; we'll cover this in a later chapter.

15
What characterizes anxious attachment in relationships?

Our anxiously attached relationships are characterized by the impact of low self-esteem and self-worth and the constant concern that others will not reciprocate our love. We crave intimacy but also remain anxious about whether our partner is able and willing to meet our emotional needs, even when they prove their love for us over and over again. Autonomy and independence in relationships can make us feel anxious. In addition, interpreting our partner's behavior patterns as insincere or inconsistent activates our attachment wound.

Anxious attachment shows up in our relationships in a variety of ways:

- ➢ Needing constant contact and support from our partner
- ➢ A constant need for reassurance that we are good enough
- ➢ Hypersensitivity to rejection and abandonment
- ➢ Negative self-view and self-worth
- ➢ Being overly sensitive to other's actions and moods
- ➢ Difficulty setting boundaries, often infringing on the boundaries of others
- ➢ The impulse to fix, save or caretake
- ➢ Being afraid or incapable of being alone
- ➢ Ruminating and over-analyzing the small things
- ➢ Catastrophizing

16
How does anxious attachment show up in our relationships?

Anxious attachment appears in our relationships in many forms, but the most prominent sign is a deep fear of abandonment and rejection. This fear produced many coping mechanisms, most of which have become so ingrained in us that we consider them normal personality traits.

Never saying no. Self-neglect is a survival strategy to keep love in our lives. As anxious attachers, we tend to say 'yes' to things we don't agree with or don't want. If, as children, we didn't get consistent love and attention, then we learned to perform or work for love. This often meant hiding our true selves and needs to please a parent figure and be an easy child. This pattern is carried into our adult relationships, where we struggle to say 'no' due to an internalized fear of rejection. We believe that being agreeable means being lovable, so we people-please, we always say yes, we volunteer to help, fix or save.

Not setting boundaries. The lack of boundaries shows up in adult relationships more than we notice. Most of us with anxious attachment don't know how to set or respect healthy boundaries. Have you ever caught yourself not telling your partner that their behavior causes you much pain and anxiety? Or perhaps you crossed your partner's boundaries by repeatedly doing something that triggers them. Healthy boundaries are there to protect us. They are the halfway point between how much we can love and respect ourselves and our partners. Setting boundaries isn't selfish or demanding; however, anxiously attached people find it incredibly hard because they grew up having to neglect them to get closer to their parent figure.

Pretending to be okay. Masking our mental state and feelings is another coping mechanism for the anxiously attached. This developed as a response to consistently not having our needs met in early childhood. We learned not to share our needs or ask for what we want. This behavior resurfaces in our adult relationships, where we don't speak our needs and don't want to appear disagreeable. Instead, we follow our partner's plan or way of living, molding ourselves into the person we think they would like. This is highly detrimental to the relationship, as it gives our partner an inauthentic version of us that we must live up to. Eventually, this builds up so much resentment that our unexpressed needs come back in anger outbursts, nagging, or nitpicking.

Assuming instead of asking. One of the most common problems I encounter is that people are afraid to ask their partner to clarify their thoughts or behavior. Instead, they use their imagination to fill in the blanks, making wild assumptions about even the most innocent situation. Catastrophizing is a prevalent anxious trait. Research suggests that when children are subjected to trauma in the long term, they develop an overactive amygdala. Amygdala is the part of our brain responsible for processing emotions. It is activated when we encounter a threat or perceived threat, and it contributes to outsetting our fight, flight, or freeze responses. For those children who were subjected to neglect and abuse and had to learn to fend for themselves in one way or another, this part remained overactive even in their adult years. That is why some may be more inclined to catastrophize in a threatening situation. This can look like noticing our partner acting differently, and instead of asking what the reason for the change is, we make up stories that usually reflect negatively on us.

Developing an over-focus on the partner. A lot of anxious attachers exhibit an over-focus on the partner. As children, if our needs weren't consistently met, we had to learn to 'survive' by adapting to our environment. In this case, we developed an over-focus on the parent or caregiver. This helped us decide when and how to approach them with our needs. As adults, anxious attachers tend to place an overfocus on their partner in order to get closer and build a connection. This can look like taking care of their needs, giving them extra attention, or going along with all their plans without question. While a healthy interdependent relationship relies on both partners working to meet each other's needs, an anxious attachment relationship can be rather one-sided. The anxious partner often gives beyond their means, with the other partner either not noticing this or simply leaning into the situation comfortably. This can quickly reverse and escalate, building up tension and resentment in the relationship.

Not speaking our needs. As children, we learned to put ourselves second while developing an over-focus on the parent. Consequently, we learned that our needs and wants don't matter and started placing ourselves after everyone else. By default, in our adult relationships, we put our partners first and neglect to speak up for ourselves. This behavior is usually accompanied by a number of insecurities. We fear speaking our needs because we think that stating them or expressing a boundary will make us appear needy or difficult. The truth is that there are no needy people, only people with unmet needs.

Thinking that we are difficult to handle. As anxiously attached, we are unaware of how our unchecked activating strategies can trigger our protest behaviors. This makes us think we are demanding, needy, clingy, argumentative, and irrational. This is often mirrored back to us through our partners, especially if we don't understand that unspoken and unmet needs activate anxiously attached wounds and show up as adult tantrums. When we encounter a threat or perceived threat – usually by thinking that our partner is rejecting or abandoning us – we get activated. This means that we lose control over our thoughts and behavior to the point where we are completely preoccupied with our partner and our relationship until we reestablish contact with our attachment figure (our partner). We cannot think about anything else; we put our partner on a pedestal, idealize our relationship and believe this is our only chance at love. If the conflict resolves, our nervous system gets regulated, and we return to normal. If not, we try to reestablish the connection with our partner through protest behaviors. These can be anything from excessive phone calls and text messages to picking fights, threatening to leave the relationship, or giving our partner the cold shoulder. These behaviors might come across as childish or difficult, but they all reflect an unmet need and a core wound from childhood.

17
The roles we assume in our partners' lives

With anxious attachment, we often assume the roles of savior, fixer, and caretaker. Trying to help others is natural and can come from a place of good, but with anxious attachment, we often try to save people from their own problems, navigate their lives and fix their issues, even when there is no need for this. We unconsciously try to prove our worth in a relationship; therefore, we often choose people who need saving, fixing, or taking care of. This can reach a point where we are more focused on fixing our person than accepting and loving them for who they are. These different roles we assume work as a protective shield, as we often use them to keep tabs on our partner or the relationship and control the outcome of our day-to-day challenges.

Fixer - in this role, we fix our partner's flaws and try to perfect them, hoping to mold them into the perfect version of themselves. This starts with us choosing partners who need us and putting them on a pedestal, embellishing them with outstanding but imagined traits. Then we work towards helping our partners achieve these traits by fixing who they are, how they act and react, respond, and live their lives. This doesn't actually help our partners and doesn't take into consideration their personalities or needs. This allows us to control the outcome of situations and our lives with them.

Saviour - the savior role's primary purpose is to save the partner from others, circumstances, and themselves. We do this by providing a safe space for them, sheltering them from uncomfortable situations, unwanted interactions, or negative experiences. This is very much of an overprotective mother role, where the aim is to establish a safe space at the expense of letting the partner experience their lives, connect with their friends, or solve their problems.

Caretaker - another mothering role, except in this one, we care for our partner's every need, allowing them to lean comfortably into the relationship. We clean the house, prepare the meals, take care of the children, allowing our significant other to enjoy their lives, taking over all the responsibilities from them. This eventually builds up tension and resentment in the relationship, leading to dissatisfaction and conflict. The irony of the situation is that the anxious partner will eventually get fed up and start complaining, with the other partner not understanding the sudden change.

18
What does it feel like to have an anxious attachment style?

Often worrying about being rejected or abandoned by our partner	Frequently trying to please and gain the approval of our partner
Feeling threatened, angry, jealous, or worried that our partner no longer wants us when we spend time apart	Using subtle ways of manipulation and gaslighting to stay close to our partner, or to get them to do what we want
Overreacting to things that we see as being a threat to the relationship	Wanting closeness and intimacy in a relationship, but worrying about whether we can trust or rely on our partner
Choosing partners who need fixing, saving, or taking care of, or partners who cannot commit	Overly fixating on the relationship to the point where it consumes much of our life
Fearing infidelity and abandonment	Tying our self-worth in with relationships
Constantly needing attention and reassurance from others	Having difficulty setting and respecting boundaries

19
The anxious attachment spectrum

All attachment styles happen on a spectrum from extreme to mild and knowing where we currently are will help immensely in the healing process. Remember that we all start our healing journey at different points and that it doesn't matter where we are. It isn't a reflection on our value, simply a guide to help identify the work ahead.

Extreme levels of anxious attachment are at the bottom end of the spectrum, with little awareness of relationship dynamics and how one contributes to them. Being on the lower end of the spectrum might mean that these people are highly volatile in their relationships, alternating between anger and frustration and withdrawal, which can come across as avoidance.

People with extreme anxious attachment:

➤ Have no awareness of their part in the relationship dynamic or problems
➤ Are highly controlling and manipulative
➤ Alternate between anger and withdrawal in romantic relationships when triggered
➤ Overly identify with the victim role, believing that things are done to them, and they suffer the consequences of others' actions
➤ Over-explain themselves and talk excessively, oversharing is a common issue here
➤ Have frequent highs and lows, mood swings, and conflicting opinions about their partner and their relationship

Being **high** on the anxious attachment spectrum suggests some awareness of the relational dynamic, but shows a general lack of capacity or willingness to take part in identifying or solving issues. This is where most people start getting interested in attachment style work and healing, they reach out for support and start getting familiar with their attachment style, but in most cases, they still alternate between reassurance and doubt when it comes to relationship stability, doubting whether they even made a good choice in their partner.

People with high anxious attachment:

➢ Show hyper-awareness of the partner's mood changes and shifts in reaction or behavior, are hypervigilant to other's moods and the shifts of dynamics in the relationship

➢ Exhibit very little flexibility in identifying relationship problems, or being part of the solution

➢ Are desperate to be heard or understood, but lack the tools to achieve it and communicate their problems or needs to their partner effectively and in a healthy manner

➢ Show inconsistency in trusting the partner, alternating between frequent ups and downs, and doubts about whether their partner or relationship is the right decision

A **moderate** anxious attachment style is the most common of all, and is generally characterized by high awareness and willingness, but the lack of tools to problem solve. People usually start seeing their part of the relationship dynamic at this level and communicate it to their partner. However, when the partner doesn't have a supportive reaction to this, they fall back into anxiety and start doubting themselves, as well as the partner and the relationship.

People with moderate anxious attachment:

➢ Are beginning to see their part of the problem and the relationship dynamic but are confused about what to do, alternating between overly relying on the partner for a solution to blaming themselves

➢ Are more capable of disengaging during conflict and making sense of the partner's reaction, but are failing to see how to move things forward

➢ Are starting to verbalize needs, but uncertain of their impact, and of the right way to express themselves, believing that their partner will not understand them, or will not want to problem-solve together

A **mild** anxious attachment is at the top end of the spectrum and is the easiest to heal. It is characterized by high awareness, the willingness and capacity to problem solve, and the ability to recognize triggers and self-soothe in conflict.

People with a mild anxious attachment:

➢ Can recognize their part of the problem and offer a solution or a way to meet their partner halfway
➢ Can take comfort and soothing offered by their partner, can rely on them, and practice healthy co-regulation
➢ Can and do face and verbalize feelings and fears, without holding back or fearing that it'll harm their relationship
➢ Can communicate their triggers and reactions more softly, taking into account their partner's triggers, attachment style, and relationship needs
➢ Can self-soothe and reconnect with the partner during and after conflict, with a positive outlook on moving forward

20
Common anxiously attached dating patterns

With anxious attachment we exhibit several patterns when we choose partners, when we date them, when and how we form connections, and how we manage and maintain the relationship with them. Learning about some of the most common anxiously attached dating patterns will help you recognize your own and help you make better decisions.

Choosing unavailable partners

When we choose our partners in our adult relationships, we often subconsciously repeat our old, dysfunctional family dynamics. That's the reason we might be attracted to partners who are emotionally unavailable or show little willingness to commit. One of the reasons for being attracted to avoidants partners is that we, anxious attachers, **see stability and balance in them,** something that we didn't receive as children. Many avoidants come across as well-put-together, balanced, and confident people, which is appealing to the anxious person who might be striving for that influence in their life. Another reason is that an avoidantly attached person seeks disconnection to feel safe in the relationship. It's their way to cope with the trauma of being neglected or left alone with their emotions as children. **This is often a cue for the anxious person to help fix, save, and care for the avoidant partner.** As many ambivalent people assume caretaking roles, they feel they are given a sense of importance in the relationship.

Attaching prematurely

We attach prematurely because we are disconnected from ourselves and have unhealed childhood wounds that we simply keep ignoring. So we hide the shame and heartbreak, the feeling of inadequacy, and pour all that we have into the new partner, hoping they won't notice the real us.

This mask works against us as our unhealed traumas and unaddressed attachment wounds resurface whether we want them or not. Even when we start a relationship by 'proving our worth' and making ourselves invaluable in the partner's life, our attachment and consequent coping behaviors will emerge sooner or later. We only attach prematurely until we realize our self-worth and decide to look for the right match instead of settling and mending.

Craving closeness very early on

Craving intimacy and being emotionally or physically close to your loved ones is a human need. Being loved and cared for in a relationship is our preferred state, so it's no wonder we crave that closeness from the get-go. However, for the anxiously attached, this urge starts at the early stages of dating. We feel the urge to get to know our partners well, have them let us in, get under their skin and learn all there is to know about them from the start. One contributing factor to this is **our abandonment wound.** We feel the need to be accepted, the need to be chosen by someone. We need external reassurance that we are good and worthy of love.

Putting our partner on a pedestal

Getting to know someone new is a fantastic feeling, especially at the beginning stages of a relationship. We admire their outstanding qualities, enjoy their company, and can't get enough of them. The problem usually begins when we forget that this person is another imperfect human, and we start idealizing them, embellishing them with imagined qualities, amplifying their good traits, and neglecting to see the bad. This is a lose-lose situation for both partners for many reasons.

When we put our partners on a pedestal, we:

- ➢ Create an idea of them that doesn't necessarily match reality
- ➢ Make an **unhealthy comparison** between the partner and ourselves, further depleting our self-worth
- ➢ Create an image of them that is **unattainable**, pushing ourselves even further from the partner
- ➢ **Put a lot of pressure on the partner** to live up to these fantasy qualities, leading to misunderstandings in the relationship

➤ **Create an impossible standard** for the partner to live up to because we dismiss their flaws

Being sensitive and hyper-vigilant to any emotional unavailability

We go head first into relationships, giving a lot to our partners. So no wonder we get disappointed if our affections or the intensity of our feelings are not reciprocated. So we become anxious about our partner's emotional reciprocity and hyper-vigilant about their mood shifts, responses, and reactions.

Emotionally unavailable people are difficult to spot, especially in the early stages of the relationship. They can be charming, engaging, and make us feel like they are committed. They may even be physically available at all times. But as time passes and the relationship deepens, something inside us begins to feel lonely and dissatisfied, and we are not sure why.

Here are some of the signs of someone who is emotionally closed off and unavailable:

➤ They hardly share how they feel, their response is usually a simple "I'm okay"
➤ It takes a long time to get to know them, their feelings, and their thoughts
➤ They have the tendency to turn sensitive or emotionally charged topics into a joke
➤ They are usually conflict avoidant and dismissive, shutting down discussions quickly
➤ They may mock you or call you out on being too sensitive
➤ They can only engage in a certain level of emotional connection and might try to make you feel guilty for wanting more

➤ They might be passive and distant

➤ When you share something in more depth, they seem to check out or have to distract themselves

➤ They try to tone down your excitement or joy, telling you to 'calm down' or 'cheer up' in intense situations

➤ They hardly ever show genuine enthusiasm for your plans or ideas

➤ They generally avoid talking about their childhood

Being full of worry and doubt about the future of the relationship, especially in the early stages

This is very common with anxious attachment. As exciting as the beginning stage of a relationship can be, it also increases a lot of worries, tied in with our most profound insecurities. We often think, what if they don't like us? What if they date around or keep their options open? In the early stages of dating, a widespread feeling of anxious attachment is reaching for connection. It can show up as overwhelming concern about a potential partner's text response time, feeling emotionally out of control when we haven't heard from someone we want to, or constant rumination over our conversations and what they mean. It can show up in many ways—most notably as emotional distress over feelings of uncertainty.

Tendency to overshare in the hope of bringing the partner closer

Oversharing is a tendency to say more than is appropriate in a given situation or to a specific person. One of the reasons for oversharing is that we hope to build emotional intimacy before we are ready or the situation allows it. This can often be connected to anxiety or a fear of not being liked by the person. With anxious attachment, oversharing is a prevalent 'tactic,' partly because we want to bring our date closer and make them understand why we do what we do.

This can be incredibly intense for the other person making us feel vulnerable and regretful.

21
How do we act in relationships with an anxious attachment?

We exhibit specific unconscious behaviors in relationships to stay close to our partners and maintain our 'importance' in their lives. These behaviors are coping mechanisms developed in early childhood and can be the result of the internalized shame of 'not being good enough,' of not learning healthy communication techniques in our childhood, and of not knowing how to express our feelings.

We are clingy. To be clingy means to stay highly close to or dependent on someone for emotional support and a sense of security. This means we need constant contact and reassurance to feel connected to our partner. This often means we disrespect our partner's boundaries or make them feel bad for taking time out of the relationship.

We can get irrationally jealous. Jealousy is part of life; a healthy amount comes up even in secure relationships. But with anxious attachment, we can be so preoccupied with the availability of our partner that we pay too much attention to their patterns and can become irrationally jealous if we find something out of character. Research has found that people's attachment styles influence how they experience jealousy in their partnerships. Anxiously attached people experience more anger and irritability. They are more likely to engage in surveillance behavior and are hypervigilant to cues of rejection or perceived threats to their relationship.

We often micromanage our partners' lives in an effort to make ourselves invaluable and a 'great asset' to the relationship. This also gives us a sense of control over our partnerships, predicting the outcome of most situations and making us feel safer and more secure in the relationship.

We go from 0 to 100 in a matter of minutes. We've all experienced problems that were so overwhelming that we just couldn't control our reaction and let things get out of hand pretty quickly. This is very common for the anxiously attached, for we didn't learn to effectively regulate our own emotions and soothe ourselves as children. We grew up in a constant turbulence of emotions and have learned that ups and downs are normal. At the same time, we have a lot of underlying anger, frustration, and resentment, and these resurface when our core wound gets triggered.

We assume the roles of savior, fixer, and caretaker. Trying to help others is natural and can come from a place of good, but with anxious attachment, we often try to save people from their own problems. We unconsciously try to prove our worth in a relationship; therefore, we choose people who we can save, fix, or who need taking care of. This can get to a point where we are more focused on fixing our person than accepting and loving them for who they are.

We believe that we need to work hard to be loved. If we grew up thinking that love is conditional, then we likely learned to audition or work hard to get it. This behavior is carried into our adult relationships, where we tend to think we need to earn our partner's love and affection. That's why we often end up putting more effort into our partnerships than our significant others.

We show manipulative behaviors. Those of us with anxious attachment are more likely to engage in manipulative behaviors to prevent our partner from leaving the relationship. We may also use manipulative techniques to have our needs met or control the outcome of certain situations. These can look like gaslighting our partner, stonewalling, or threatening to leave the relationship when we have no intention to do so.

22
How does being clingy show up in our relationships?

To be clingy means we need to stay highly close to or dependent on someone for emotional support and a sense of security. This means we need constant contact, reassurance, and validation to feel connected to our partner. This often means we disrespect our partner's boundaries or make them feel bad to want to take time out of the relationship.

Being clingy develops as a protective mechanism to having our needs inconsistently met in childhood. We begin internalizing that love and attention are conditional and grow up believing we cannot expect them from others. This is because we didn't learn the concept of emotional permanence, which is the assured feeling of being loved, regardless of external conditions, e.g., without our loved ones present. If we don't learn this as kids, we need constant reassurance from our partners, letting us know we are loved and cared for.

Being clingy in the relationship looks like

- Not giving the partner space or alone time, especially if they have specifically requested it
- Calling or texting the other nonstop when we're not together, expecting an instant response, panicking if your partner does not respond to texts or calls
- Rushing the relationship, attaching prematurely, moving in prematurely, or moving too fast in the partnership
- Deceptively creating an image of ourselves that your partner finds attractive, emphasizing our positive traits but mainly hiding the negative ones. Anxious attachers tend to mold themselves into the perfect version of what they think their partner wants

➤ Trying to force a partner to love us, asking them if they do so over and over and if the response is not favorable, using manipulation techniques to make them feel bad

➤ Attempting to earn someone's love by doing things they like, assuming the role of the perfect girlfriend

➤ Asking for reassurance often or frequently asking our partner if they love us

➤ Looking for cues of being rejected or betrayed and using subtle ways of manipulation to avoid it

➤ Controlling behaviors, such as wanting to track our significant other's location on our phones

23
Anxious attachment and jealousy

Jealousy is part of life and even securely attached people experience it to a certain level, but with anxious attachment we are often so insecure, that we project our fearful and anxious thoughts onto our relationships, believing that we are not good enough, or that we don't deserve love. This makes us more prone to believe that our partner will reject, abandon us, or leave us for someone better.

Research has found that people's attachment styles influence how they experience jealousy in their partnerships. Anxiously attached people experience more anger and irritability, are more likely to engage in surveillance behavior, and are hypervigilant to cues of rejection or perceived threats to their relationship.

Different types of jealousy:

Inducing jealousy - Anxiously attached people are more likely to induce jealousy in their relationship to ensure a reaction from their partner. This reaction helps confirm their partner's feelings, reduce their anxiety, and even boost their self-esteem.

Engaging in surveillance behavior - Anxious folks are more likely to engage in surveillance behavior, monitoring their partner's physical or online whereabouts. This can include checking their phone, emails, calling them randomly and checking where they are, checking in with friends to confirm the partner's story checks out, quizzing their children about their mom/dad's movements during the day, or even physically stalking them.

Jealousy caused by low self-esteem - This type of jealous behavior is caused by the low self-worth of the anxiously attached person. It can be triggered by the partner looking at other people, having a good relationship with close friends or colleagues, or simply shifting the attention in the relationship elsewhere. It is deeply rooted in how the anxious partner values themselves and is often followed by thoughts of catastrophizing, believing that the partner has an affair or will leave them simply because they will find someone better.

24
Manipulative techniques and anxious attachment

Those of us with anxious attachment are more likely to engage in manipulative behaviors to prevent our partner from leaving the relationship. **One way our anxious attachment style impacts our relational behavior is by influencing our relationship maintenance strategies, which are behaviors we use to keep our partners closer and make our relationships last.** According to research, people with anxious attachment are more prone to engaging in mate retention strategies intended to prevent the partner from leaving and bring them closer. Cost-inflicting mate retention strategies include stalking the partner online, checking their phones, or trying to make them jealous, while benefit-provisioning strategies are complimenting the partner, craving closeness to them, or showing them affection.

This finding suggests that we use subtle manipulative techniques to meet our needs or control the outcome of certain situations. These tactics can look like gaslighting our partner, stonewalling, or threatening to leave the relationship when we do not intend to.

Some of the most common manipulative techniques are

➢ **Shaming.** Attempting to change or influence the feelings of someone by constantly subjecting them to shame or guilt. This is often used to divert attention from things or people that the partner likes or enjoys in order to focus the extra time on us: "Those video games you always play are childish and a complete waste of time."

➢ **Having unreasonable expectations** of our partner, e.g., expecting them to always be at our back and call or always agree with us and validate our opinion

➢ **Passive-aggressiveness.** This happens when someone says or indicates something without outright saying what they mean. There are many forms this can take, including sarcasm, pouting, or even giving the silent treatment. This is intended to keep the other person second-guessing, diverting attention from being able to evaluate their feelings in the relationship.

➢ **Name-calling.** Refusing to show respect, shaming the partner, calling them out on their behavior in front of others, and calling them names. The purpose of this is to make them believe they are less than others and or that they are not worthy of better treatment. This might start small, then increase in frequency or intensity over time.

➢ **Projection** is a psychological defense mechanism where a person tries to avoid facing their issues or insecurities by putting their feelings, desires, or characteristics on another person.

➢ **Guilt tripping** happens when someone is made to feel bad for minor things. Guilt gives the offender a sense of control over the victim, as guilt is a powerful emotion that makes people more agreeable or compliant. This tactic influences or dominates the partner: "If you really loved me, you would go out of your way for me."

➤ **Moving the goalpost.** This happens when someone constantly changes the criteria their partner must meet to satisfy them. For example, suggesting that their partner spends too much time with their friends, and it negatively impacts their relationship. Then when the partner cuts back on this, they start suggesting that the partner works too much or spends too much time with their family.

Emotional manipulation techniques happen mostly unconsciously in an effort the keep our partner in our lives. However, they have a severe negative impact on our partner and our partnership. All of us are guilty of using specific manipulative techniques from time to time, often unknowingly and without deliberately trying to damage the partnership. So when identifying your behavior, practice compassion and remember that these tactics show up even in healthy relationships to some degree. The sooner you recognize them, the sooner you can correct them.

25
What does it sound like to have an anxious attachment?

I want to be close to you, but I'm not sure you want to be emotionally close to me.	I always want to be with or in contact with you.
I don't feel complete when I'm single or alone.	My insecurities make me jealous.
I feel anxious about whether our relationship will last.	I need constant reassurance of your love and commitment.

I question whether you love me as much as I love you.	I've been told I am needy and high-maintenance.
I wonder if something is wrong with me that makes you pull away.	I can't tolerate uncertainty in our relationship.
Little things like not answering your phone make me anxious, and question your love for me.	I keep comparing myself to others, thinking I am less than them.
I don't feel I am worth much.	I worry you will leave me.
I'm not good enough to deserve a healthy relationship.	I am too needy and high-maintenance for anyone to put up with me.
I am jealous of your friends because you seem to have a better time with them than with me.	If I feel anxious about our relationship, I may start doing something to get your attention.

26
What happens when our anxious attachment gets activated?

Suppose we grew up in a family where our needs were inconsistently met, where we learned to work for love and attention, or assumed roles of fixing and caretaking. In that case, we inevitably develop certain coping mechanisms to help us navigate the dysfunctional dynamics, bring us closer to our attachment figures, and work through the difficulties of not getting the attention, love, and validation we need. However, these circumstances may also resurface in our adult partnerships, and just like in childhood, our attachment system gets activated as a response.

Activating strategies are our brain's way of soothing us when we feel disconnected from our attachment figure, in this case, our partner. Once the connection is reestablished, these strategies go away and stop until we are activated again. When our attachment system gets activated, we start constantly thinking about our partner with great difficulty focusing on anything else, putting our partner on a pedestal, remembering only their outstanding qualities, fantasizing about them coming back to us, or thinking they are the one. When activated, we have difficulties focusing on anything else due to our preoccupation with the attachment figure. If soothed effectively, we return to a regulated nervous system. However, if the connection isn't reestablished, we will start exhibiting certain protest behaviors to try to reconnect with our partner.

27
What are the anxiously attached protest behaviors?

If we are activated, and our attachment figure responds negatively to our distress, then our anxious attachment triggers protest behaviors in us. These protest behaviors range from becoming distant to testing our partners. They also vary from person to person based on our temperament, the relationship, where we are on the anxious attachment spectrum, etc.

The most common protest behaviors are:

Trying to make our partner jealous. We induce jealousy because we need confirmation that our partner cares for us, and we want them to prove this. This behavior can play out in flirting, posting on social media, or making comparisons with our ex-partners.

Becoming clingy. We want to reestablish that closeness as soon as possible, so we lean heavily into the relationship. We crave more security than others, and we fear that either physical or emotional distance will make us drift further apart. This behavior goes hand in

THE ANXIOUS ATTACHMENT HANDBOOK

hand with rushing things in the relationship, like moving in too early with the partner or expecting their affirmation of love too soon.

Picking fights. This may happen because we need assurance of our partner's love, and if they fight back with us, it confirms that. Another reason for this behavior is that fighting creates heightened emotions that feel natural to the anxiously attached. This is our version of love, as we have likely identified the love and emotional closeness with dysregulation and intensity.

Testing. We exhibit several testing behaviors because we feel insecure and need confirmation that our partner still loves us, cares for us, and won't abandon us. These testing behaviors come up in various ways, including pulling away, false threats, withholding contact, going into avoidance, or purposefully taking a long time to respond to a text or phone call.

Pushing our partners away without wanting them to go away. This is reversed psychology, as by pulling out, we actually want our partner to come towards us. We want them to chase because it gives our inner child the validation of being loved and wanted. This is a form of testing that we use when we are in separation from our attachment figures.

28
Why are we triggered by peace?

Peace, particularly the balance and calm of a relationship, can be incredibly triggering for the anxiously attached. It feels unnatural and makes us think that there is cause for concern. It awakens our suspicion, making us believe there must be something wrong with the relationship. It makes us question our partner's love for us simply because our idea of love is often the opposite of balance.

One of the reasons for this is that if we were raised on a roller coaster of emotions, we would become triggered by peace simply because the chaotic emotions we grew up with have

become the norm, and everything else feels frightening. That's why we subconsciously crave partners who create uncertainty, reject us, or are chaotic in their ways. We unconsciously recreate our childhood patterns and let our brains recycle old wounds.

Another possible reason is that we learned to identify love with a set of inconsistent behaviors, frequent ups and downs, and an imbalance of emotional availability. So when coupled up with a partner who is emotionally available, expressive, and relaxed about relationship needs, we tend to view it as unusual at best.

29
What is our biggest fear with anxious attachment?

Our biggest fear in a romantic relationship is to be rejected or abandoned. It rules our emotions, actions, and reactions and makes us preoccupied with our partners' behaviors. This fear is so intense that it comes up even in a loving and caring relationship. Suppose we grew up in a home where love, attention, and affection from a parent weren't readily available. We likely internalized this as the norm, believing it applies to all other relationships. As an additional defensive technique, we may have tried to earn love and affection by performing or auditioning. This happened because the message we received was that we weren't worthy otherwise.

As adults, we unconsciously recreate the past and consequently may not end up in a healthy relationship dynamic but repeat the parent-child pattern we grew up with, even when we consciously know it's not good for us. This further fuels our fear of rejection, as we often end up choosing partners who are similar to our caregivers in emotional availability, responsiveness, or behavior. This serves as a self-fulfilling prophecy that reiterates the original fear and behavior dynamic.

30
How do we approach our problems with anxious attachment?

For someone who is anxiously attached, relationship problems are blown out of proportion, and emotions around them are heightened. When triggered, we start seeing things through the lens of our attachment system. So simple problems become the question of 'I'm not lovable,' 'They don't care for me,' or 'They will never love me the way I want to be loved.' This catastrophizing thinking pattern is rooted in our internalized shame and our insecurities about not being good enough. It makes us act unpredictably, nag about the small things, or hold onto grudges. It doesn't make any problem go away, not to mention it creates more tension as our partners don't always understand what is behind our often extreme reactions.

31
How do we communicate with anxious attachment?

Our earliest experience with relationships is witnessing our parents or caregivers being in one. This forms our view of what a relationship dynamic looks like, even if this dynamic is not the healthiest. We soak up our parents' communication styles, expressions of mood, body language, and how they relate to one another. We learn – or don't – how relationships work through our parents. We develop several communication techniques, some of which can erode our partnerships in the long run.

With anxious attachment, we use a number of these dysfunctional communication techniques, and very often, we don't realize how they impact the narrative of what we are trying to relay or the dynamic between us and our partner. Anxiously attached people are generally open and willing to share vulnerably with their partners. They don't have problems opening up to discuss relationship issues; they prefer solving them rather than letting things fester. However, they don't always choose the best tools to express their distress or ask for their needs or wants. Here are some of the most common dysfunctional communication techniques that come up for a lot of us:

Criticizing

Criticizing our partner when they can't meet our emotional needs is very common in anxious attachment communication. We do this to avoid coming across as needy or demanding. Instead of communicating the real problem, we deflect and start bringing up our partner's faults or past mistakes in both big and small ways; however, we unconsciously try to let our partner know that we need more attention, reassurance, or validation.

Being needy

We tend to be clingy and needy in relationships as a way to get closer to our partners. We call and text them excessively to establish a connection, and this gets pushed to unhealthy extremes. This usually happens when we feel that our partner either emotionally or physically pulls away. We go into a panicked frenzy, not knowing how to reconnect. So we smother them in attention instead of asking for the reason for the disconnect or giving them space to regulate their emotions.

Nitpicking

Nitpicking is the tendency to look for minor faults or mistakes in our partners and bring them up in response to a situation we can't or don't want to address directly. For example, we are arguing with our partners over something we asked them to do. We can't seem to get our way because the partner is unresponsive or unwilling to solve the problem, so instead of expressing how disappointed we are, we start bringing up their faults or past mistakes.

Stonewalling

This happens when in a discussion or argument, one partner withdraws from the conversation, shutting down and physically or mentally distancing themselves from the other. This might be their response to feeling overwhelmed; metaphorically speaking, they pull up a wall around them. Stonewalling can show up by giving the silent treatment, rolling the eyes, looking away from the partner, acting busy, and ignoring the conversation altogether.

Shaming

By shaming, we try to make our partners look bad and shift the blame, suggesting they are the problem, not us. Shaming can come out in many forms, from calling the partner too dramatic, too needy, or having little empathy to directly shaming them in front of friends or family by calling attention to something they lack or did wrong.

Projecting

Projecting is a defensive technique we use to project traits or habits we don't like in ourselves to our partner. This works like taking our problem or insecurity and making it sound like our partner's fault. It can sound like, "You are the problem, not me," or "You probably cheated on me; that's why you act weird."

Keeping score

We keep score to avoid addressing issues and shift the blame onto the partner by putting one on them. In the heat of the argument, we often don't respond to the topic at hand but bring up something painful the partner did to us.

Deflecting

Deflecting means consistently distracting from the problem and shifting blame to the partner. Deflecting is a way to avoid the negative consequences of any actions while blaming others. Deflecting can feel dismissive and inconsiderate as the partner who engages in this technique minimizes the other's feelings, steering away from dealing with the problem at hand.

32
What are our strengths with anxious attachment?

So far, we have talked mainly about the negatives. Still, there are heaps of remarkable traits that make anxiously attached people great, and the first and probably most outstanding is our ability to feel deeply and empathize with others, accompanied by significant emotional awareness.

As anxious attachers, we are:

- ➢ Emotionally expressive, making it much easier for us to talk about our feelings and problems
- ➢ Loyal and devoted partners and friends, those close to us can always count on us
- ➢ Attuned to our friends' and partners' emotional needs, as we value great connection in a relationship
- ➢ Good at talking about our relationship concerns and open to solving them
- ➢ Not shy when it comes to supporting and praising others
- ➢ Able to empathize with the problems of others, and can hold space for their pain and struggle, even if we are hurting too

33
How do we choose partners with anxious attachment?

With anxious attachment, we unconsciously repeat childhood patterns and choose partners based on the family dynamics we grew up with. If we grew up in a home where love, attention, and affection from a parent weren't readily available, we most likely learned to earn it by performing or auditioning for it. We received the message that love wasn't unconditional but something we had to work for, so in our adult relationships, we audition or work extra hard to be loved. Or perhaps, we grew up with an emotionally unavailable parent who abandoned us. Hence, as adults, we reenact this core wound by choosing partners who exhibit similar behaviors, like being closed off or unwilling to commit. **As adults, we live out internalized childhood beliefs by not engaging in healthy relationships but repeating the same parent-child dynamic that is familiar to us, even when we consciously know we deserve better.** That's why we often go for avoidant partners or people that are emotionally unavailable, closed off, dismissive, or need fixing or saving.

34
Why do we attach prematurely?

Attaching prematurely is very common with anxious attachment. We start fantasizing about a future together when we meet someone new. We embellish them with exceptional traits and fill in the blanks before we get to know them. **We attach prematurely because we are disconnected from ourselves and have unhealed childhood wounds that we don't want to pay attention to.** Attaching prematurely is most likely the result of abandonment in childhood, where our parent or caregiver wasn't emotionally available for us, so we had to make up for their lack of love and affection in our imagination. We may have idolized the parent and created a loving and caring persona around them as a way of self-preservation.

This gets pushed out into our adult relationships, where we long for the right connection so much that we create it in our minds. We easily ignore the reality of things, red flags, or the real personality of the people we date, and create an almost false persona around them, so they meet our expectations – at least in our imagination – and can fulfill our needs for the perfect partner. Then we get attached to them before we even know who they are. This attachment serves as a shield, making us feel chosen and wanted, which was probably lacking in our childhood. However, attaching prematurely can easily backfire, preventing us from assessing each potential partner, and focusing on long-term compatibility and shared values, instead of chemistry and a great connection.

How does anxious attachment impact our relationships?

35
Becoming aware of your anxious attachment

A common theme I see with anxiously attached people is that they're either unaware of their attachment style or don't know how it impacts their relationships. Many anxiously attached people have no idea how their attachment style developed. They had loving and caring parents and a perfect childhood. But in reality, our brain has a pesky way of deleting and blocking traumatic experiences, and some information gets completely erased. So how do we start recognizing our anxious attachment? **To begin the healing process, we must first become familiar with our patterns, triggers, and reactions to them.** If they are not apparent, we must find alternative information sources. Try observing your behavior, pause, and pay attention to how you react and behave. Talk to your current or ex-partner about it. Try to witness your family dynamics and your parent's communication styles. Speak to your friends. Perhaps they observed patterns that you did not pay any attention to. Try journaling about your past relational experiences. Can you spot recurring themes? Is there an overarching pattern to all of your romantic partnerships? What can you notice? Paying attention to how you choose partners, how you treat people and let them treat you will reveal a lot of important information about your relationship patterns.

36
Anxious attachment mistakes to avoid

When we first discover our attachment style, it is revealing and overwhelming at the same time. It explains our past behaviors and reactions and directly describes why and how we get triggered. However, we all encounter a few common mistakes as we get absorbed in attachment theory and discover ourselves through the lens of anxious attachment. Let's walk through the most common ones:

➤ **Overestimating our problems.** Attachment styles happen on a spectrum, meaning that some of us are on the more extreme end, while others have a mild anxious attachment. However, our attachment style is only one part of our multilayered personalities, and they don't mean that there is something fundamentally or unchangeably wrong with us. Securely attached people also experience relationship problems such as misunderstandings, feeling frustrated and unhappy, so relational problems are not only the byproduct of our attachment styles. Overestimating the problem will only hinder the healing process. When we blow our issues out of proportion, it is much easier to get overwhelmed and stand in our way by feeling sorry for ourselves, intellectualizing the problem, or procrastinating.

➤ **Blaming our parents.** As anxious attachment forms due to inconsistent parenting, it is easy to shift the blame on our parent or caregiver, often to a point where we create irreconcilable differences or completely distance ourselves from them. It's essential to remember that our parents are imperfect people, constantly battling their unresolved traumas or painful upbringing, and most likely, they did the best they could with their level of awareness and knowledge. Our anxious attachment does not directly reflect on our parents but rather our interpretation of their parenting styles.

For example, if our parent was inconsistent with us, it doesn't necessarily mean they did not love us. It could mean several things, from being inexperienced in raising a child to being overwhelmed with other responsibilities. Being a parent is an incredibly stressful and often overwhelming job, and we live multifaceted lives where we hope to do well on all fronts. Being anxiously attached doesn't necessarily mean that your parents didn't care for you or that you had a bad childhood.

➢ **Giving ourselves a label.** With attachment theory, the goal is to identify the cluster of people that needs work in this area. Our attachment explains how we see and deal with difficulties in our lives, mainly in our relationships, depending on the type of care available to us as children. It's nothing more than that. So slapping a label on it is both reductive and detrimental, as we are so much more than just someone who is anxiously attached. Other elements of our personalities play a massive part in how we see the world, and we must consider these to make an informed decision on our life or relationship choices.

➢ **Oversimplifying our attachment profile.** I often get asked, 'Can I be anxiously and avoidantly attached simultaneously?' and the answer is yes. Our attachment isn't completely black and white, as even though we have a dominant attachment style, we exhibit traits of secure, anxious, and avoidant attachment, depending on our partner, the relationship, the context or the situation, and the people we are around. This mixed attachment profile is very common, and an easy example would be that we might exhibit secure traits around our friends but are anxiously attached to our partners. Another example is that we have an anxious attachment in our relationships but need a lot of space and time alone to self-soothe as avoidantly traded people do.

➢ **Trying to diagnose others.** We've all been there. We learned all there is to know about anxious attachment, followed the relevant social media accounts, took several tests, and now call ourselves pros regarding insecure attachment styles. We look at our friends and potential partners through an attachment lens and label them as 'avoidants' or 'disorganized.' And while it's absolutely okay to wonder about or analyze our friends' or partners' attachment styles, we should not make assumptions based on this, draw consequences about their personalities, or try to predict their future reactions.

37
What is a trigger?

Emotional triggers can be anything that causes our mind and body to react in extreme and unexpected ways, regardless of our current mood. This can include experiences, events, people, places, or things. Each triggering experience is different, determined by what causes it. A trigger can be anything that causes us to recall a traumatic experience from our past. Some common situations that cause us anxious attachers to get triggered are rejection, betrayal, being excluded or ignored, feeling unwanted, or losing a connection. It is important to mention that anxious attachers may get triggered by the perceived threat of any of the above situations. For example, our partner is asking for space, and based on our childhood experiences of neglect, we instantly jump to the conclusion that they don't love, care for, or want to be with us anymore.

38
How to recognize your trigger?

The easiest way to recognize our triggers is to pay attention to situations that generate strong emotions or bodily sensations. Emotional sensations might be crying, unexplained anger, panic, sadness, or emptiness. Physical sensations include a pounding heart, sweaty hands, dizziness, numbness, or upset stomach. If these arise unexpectedly in situations, and we cannot explain why they're there, we have a good reason to believe that our attachment trauma or a core wound is triggering us.

39
Common anxious attachment triggers

Try paying attention to your triggers. Listen to your intrusive thoughts, and pay closer attention to your emotions and reactions. How and when do they show up? Is there a recurring pattern?

Our attachment trauma is rooted in abandonment, and some of the most triggering feelings come from fear of rejection or a perceived threat to the relationship. **Here are a few things that can trigger our anxious attachment:**

Partner needing space or time alone, away from us	Inconsistent behavior we pick up on in the relationship
Partner is emotionally closed off	Refusal to commit
Physical distance	Mixed signals
Lack of open communication	Lack of transparency
Inability to solve problems	Secrets in the relationship
Partner unavailable to discuss Partner is not willing to share their feelings or solve problems	Close friendships or family ties Partner having interests outside of the relationship, that makes us feel excluded
Work commitments	Partner having hobbies
Partner chatting to someone attractive	Focus shifting outside the relationship

40
The power of our thoughts

The quality of our life is determined by the quality of our thoughts. **Our thoughts create experiences, and we experience what we think.** If we put it this way, we begin realizing that our anxious attachment is a vicious circle of getting triggered by our past trauma, attributing a negative emotion to the trigger, and acting out on the experience of an emotion that is nothing else but the remnant of our past.

Let's take anxiety as an example. Anxiety is a sudden bout of energy we feel in our body when we face a new or unexpected experience or event. We can respond in two ways, depending on how we are wired or emotionally conditioned. We can feel anxiety in the face of the new event, or we can feel excitement. This is the classic 'cup half empty, half full' philosophy.

Most of our thoughts throughout the day don't influence our behavior or cause us any harm. However, our recurring thoughts, the ones that live rent-free in our heads, can impact our perception of and the actions or reactions we take in response to them. The more we do something, the more likely we will do it again. Repetition rewires the brain and breeds habits. According to neuroscience, cells that fire together wire together, meaning the more we repeat the same thought over and over in our heads, the likelier it is to become a habit that is hard to break. We will likely do two things once we draw a conclusion about ourselves. One, we'll look for evidence to reinforce that belief; two, we'll discard any proof pointing to the contrary. That's why catching our intrusive thoughts is vital, and paying attention to our repeating thought patterns.

41
Our emotions as survival mechanisms

From a biological and evolutionary perspective, negative or distressing emotions can be categorized as survival-mode

emotions, such as fear, anger, and disgust, to mention a few. They work as a signal letting our body and brain know that we might be in danger. They are designed to motivate behaviors and bodily responses that can deal with the risks and threats we face in our environment. Research suggests that we benefit from our emotions, and each emotion has its purpose, even when negative. Fear suggests danger and prompts us to run or fight back. Anger suggests an obstacle, encouraging us to become assertive in our ways. Joy means reinforcement in our daily choices, helping to form habits.

A group of brain structures controls our emotions, called the limbic system. The limbic system releases chemicals as we react to our surroundings. Each chemical release prompts an emotion; for example, oxytocin allows us to feel love and joy, while endorphins help relieve pain, reduce stress, and improve our mood.

So when we look at our emotions as inevitable or something that kept us safe throughout evolution, it is perhaps easier to accept them as part of our biology, and it is also easier to treat them as such. Research suggests that the physiological lifespan of emotion is 90 seconds. What keeps it lingering is the story we attach to it. And it's completely normal to tell ourselves stories, as we want to justify our sensations. However, by witnessing our emotions, we enable ourselves to detach from the pain we associate with them because while pain is inevitable, suffering is optional.

42
Stress responses

Some of our triggers suggest childhood traumas that come to the surface through different stress responses. **When facing a stressor, whether a real or perceived threat, we enter into one of the four stress responses; fight, flight, freeze, or fawn.** Our stress responses are engrained survival instincts that helped our ancestors deal with dangerous situations and environments. Back then, stressors indicated life or death situations; however, in today's society, we face very different high-arousal situations that are more psychological in nature, e.g., relationship problems or job interviews.

The stress response begins in the brain. When we spot danger, our eyes or ears send information to the amygdala about the threat. The amygdala is the area of the brain that contributes to emotional processing. It interprets the images and sounds, and if it perceives danger, it instantly signals to the hypothalamus, which activates the sympathetic nervous system, and hormones get released into the bloodstream. These hormones bring on several physiological changes, including a racing heartbeat, raised blood pressure, and heavy breathing. These changes happen so quickly that we aren't even aware of them. It's so quick that it happens before we can visually take it in. That's how we are often able to react and act in danger before we even think about what to do. So we can conclude that our stress responses happen automatically before we can reason or respond. Stress responses are part of our biology; however, it is essential to understand that while they used to serve us in life-or-death situations, today, they are triggered by everyday stimuli, like a job interview, a breakup, or even the inconsistencies we pick up on in our relationships.

43
Our reactions to the different stress responses

The stress or trauma responses are usually called the 4Fs – fight, flight, freeze, and fawn. These have evolved as a survival mechanism to help us react quickly to life-threatening situations. We automatically react with one of these four trauma responses, depending on factors like individual differences and past trauma experiences.

The fight response is a more aggressive answer to the threat, where we move towards the challenge. In fight mode, we believe we can overpower the perceived threat when we notice that we are in danger. Our brain releases hormones preparing our body for a physical fight. This might feel like wanting to cry, feeling intense anger, the urge to punch or kick, or a knotted sensation in our stomach.

The flight response urges us to leave the situation. It happens when our bodies don't feel we can overcome the perceived danger but can avoid it by running away. We respond by feeling fidgety or tense, constantly shaking our legs, excessively exercising, or getting numb.

Freeze and fawn responses happen below our conscious level of understanding. This means they don't involve active decision-making; instead, they happen subconsciously.

The freeze response occurs when our body doesn't think we can fight or flight, and it causes us to be stuck in one place. The goal here is not to be noticed and to avoid being caught up in the danger of the situation. It feels like a sense of dread, pounding heart, pale skin, dissociation, numbness, exhaustion, and indecision.

The fawn response is our body's emotional reaction that involves becoming highly agreeable to the person abusing or threatening us. It is common with people who grew up experiencing abuse or had a narcissistic parent, and according to research, it is more of a learned and less of a biological reaction. It is signaled by people pleasing, being agreeable or codependent, lacking boundaries, and appeasing.

44
The healthy and unhealthy ways we use the fight response

The fight response is a natural way our nervous system reacts to a threat or perceived threat around us. Some studies suggest that those with childhood trauma have an overworking amygdala that can keep the body in constant fight mode, resulting in stress, anxiety, and depression. In healthy situations, a fight response to stress can help us in many ways. However, people with unresolved trauma may perceive everything as dangerous, leading to unhealthy fight responses. Below is a list of the healthy and unhealthy ways this shows up in our lives.

Healthy fight responses	Unhealthy fight responses
Creating boundaries	Controlling behaviors
Being assertive	Narcissistic tendencies
Finding courage	Bullying
Becoming a strong leader	Feelings of entitlement
Protecting yourself and loved ones when necessary	Demanding perfection from others

45
The healthy and unhealthy ways we use the flight response

Similar to 'fight mode,' the flight stress response happens in our body as a natural reaction to a threat or perceived threat. Essentially, our brain prepares our body to flee the situation or danger to protect ourselves. This can show up both positively and negatively in our everyday lives.

Healthy flight responses	Unhealthy flight responses
Disengaging from harmful conversations	Obsessive or compulsive tendencies
Leaving unhealthy relationships	Needing to stay busy all the time
Removing yourself from physically dangerous situations	Panic or constant fear

Properly assessing danger	Perfectionism, workaholic tendencies
Avoiding specific types of harmful behavior	Inability to sit still

46
Common physical sensations we encounter when triggered

Our reactions to triggers are diverse. We may experience bodily sensations or strong emotions such as anger, fear, anxiety, sadness, or numbness. Being triggered may primarily show up in how we behave, in forms of isolation, becoming argumentative, emotionally shut down, or even physically aggressive. Triggers can have genuine and severe consequences, so it is important to notice our trigger reactions.

Here is a list of some familiar bodily sensations we might feel when triggered:

- Headaches or migraine
- Feeling faint or dizzy
- Feeling nauseous, having an upset stomach
- Numbness in parts or the whole body
- Losing focus, losing one's voice
- Breathing difficulties
- Racing heart
- Sweaty hands or body
- A knot in the stomach or throat
- Urge to use the bathroom
- Stiff muscles
- Strong urge to cry or shout
- Shaking legs unconsciously

47
Spotting our anxiously attached patterns

Often we are so focused on finding red flags in others, that we neglect to notice our own. However, these are important indicators that we have some past trauma buried deep down, and they can guide us in finding our relationship needs, core wounds, and triggers.

Common anxiously attached patterns:

Codependency is a robust red flag in anxious attachment. Codependency in a relationship happens when one partner is mentally, emotionally, physically, or spiritually reliant on the other. A codependent relationship can exist between romantic partners but also between family members and friends. In codependent relationships, one partner tends to overly rely on the other to the point where they don't maintain a sense of self. Codependency is a behavior that we model by observing our parents, or that can be passed down intergenerationally. Codependent behaviors can severely impact our ability to create a healthy and satisfying relationship. It shows up in our emotional states, as well as our behaviors. Codependent people often form relationships that are one-sided, emotionally destructive, or even abusive.

Lacking strong interpersonal boundaries. With anxious attachment, we cannot set and enforce healthy boundaries in our relationships, and we tend to be more intrusive on our partner's emotional or physical boundaries of our partner, than other attachment styles. Boundaries define who we are and who we are not. They dictate what we allow into our lives and what we keep out. However, as anxiously attached, we grew up in environments where our boundaries often weren't respected or where we chose to 'give them up' to please our parents or caregivers. Therefore, when our partner sets or tries to reinforce their boundaries, it confuses us and triggers us instantly. It makes us feel threatened or excluded from the relationship. It is equally difficult to set our own boundaries simply because we want to please our partners and keep them close. We can also easily forgive the boundary violations of others due to our intense fear of abandonment.

Focusing on or marrying potential. We tend to focus on people's potential, as we desperately want them to be an idealized version of what we think we need instead of who they actually are. With anxious attachment, we tend to project a fantasy on our potential partners at the beginning of the dating phase. This makes us ignore their red flags and place them on a pedestal. We are so focused on finding the right person that we often embellish the people we date with traits they don't have so that we can attach to them and finally settle down. The danger in this situation is that we ignore our own needs and boundaries, thinking that with the right amount of love, our person will eventually change. Essentially, we are settling for a fantasy that we project onto our partners instead of getting to know them and deciding if they would be a great fit for us.

Being the fixer. If, in childhood, we adapt to our environment by meeting the emotional or physical needs of others and by taking care of them, then most likely, we attach a lot of meaning to being the fixer, savior, or caretaker later in our adult relationships. After all, this is how we learn to experience love and connection. We assume that our value comes from saving or fixing others instead of seeing ourselves as worthy and valuable. These traits can give us some fantastic strength. On the flip side, they inevitably build up anxiety and resentment and have the potential to break up our partnerships. Being the fixer or caretaker looks like parenting our partners, becoming their therapist, adviser, someone who keeps them in check, runs their errands, cleans their house, and makes their meals. Sadly, while doing so, we neglect to focus on our own lives and lose our sense of self in the process.

Pretending to be ok, masking our feelings. If, as children, we learned to be agreeable, to hide parts of ourselves to get closer to someone we love, and shift the focus from us to our parents, then it is likely we repeat the same dynamic in our relationships by pretending to be ok with something that is giving us anxiety. We've all been in a situation where we agreed to pick up extra errands, went to a party we didn't want to, or spent time with people we didn't like just to keep our partner happy. While healthy compromise is part of any relationship, with anxious attachment, we have a tendency to overstep our boundaries in the 'interest of the relationship.'

Being attracted to unavailable people, attracting avoidant partners, or people with dismissive behavior. Earlier relationship experiences shape our idea of what love looks like. If someone has a history of feeling abandoned, unimportant, or inadequate, they subconsciously seek relationships reinforcing those belief systems. Although these patterns are painful, they are also normal for anxious attachers. Our brain is wired to seek out what is familiar rather than what is good for us. As anxious attachers, we come from environments where our needs were inconsistently met, and we unconsciously seek out the same inconsistent behavior in our adult relationships, so we opt for emotionally unavailable partners.

Emotional unavailability is a typical pattern with avoidantly attached people, who stay in relationships as long as the emotional investment involved is not overpowering for them. The relationship stays superficially intact as long as their partner allows them to remain emotionally uninvested. Their emotional unavailability is triggered if the partner wants to grow, heal their own wounds, or invest in a more profound commitment. This is when emotionally unavailable people may become indifferent, distant, shut down, or simply discard the relationship as too much effort.

Difficulty maintaining healthy relationships. For us, anxiously attached, our deep insecurities and fear of abandonment stand in the way of holding on to and building healthy relationships. We can exhibit many behaviors that will either sabotage or slowly erode our partnerships.

➢ Violating the boundaries of our partners

- ➤ Not respecting the differences in a relationship
- ➤ Having unrealistic expectations or impossibly high standards
- ➤ Projecting our insecurities to others and acting on them impulsively
- ➤ Being passive – refusing to communicate our needs because we fear rejection
- ➤ Being controlling or possessive
- ➤ Using indirect needs to get the attention we want: picking fights, criticizing, silent treatment, withholding love
- ➤ Being overly dependent and losing our sense of self in the relationship

Deep rooted fear of abandonment and rejection. Because love was unpredictable during childhood, those of us with anxious attachment tend to seek love and approval from others and long for a deep connection. However, these childhood experiences have made it difficult to trust people close to us, including our partners. This creates overwhelming insecurity about our relationships, which may cause us to become possessive, overly dependent, and clingy toward our partners. This pushes us to constantly think we will be abandoned, left, or rejected.

Problems with self-regulation. Our early experiences with our primary caregivers play a direct role in the development of our brain, which in turn influences our ability to regulate our emotions. Insecure attachment to our caregiver in childhood results in the experience of feeling overwhelmed and unsafe, which creates hyperarousal (being on high alert) as a means of protection. Left unaddressed, this is carried into our adult lives and can significantly impact our relationships, including our relationship with ourselves. Over time these learned protective behaviors influence our reactions in relationships. In essence, if our caregiver didn't co-regulate with us, then we have no skills to downregulate negative emotions and calm our nervous system when we get triggered. This leads to the emotional turbulence and overwhelm many of us are familiar with.

Difficulty taking healthy criticism. Very few people can handle criticism graciously; for most of us, being criticized is uncomfortable or even devastating. We all need to feel good about ourselves, so the moment someone judges us negatively, any doubts we may have about ourselves can immediately catapult to the surface. Due to the lack of proper self-awareness and the inability to regulate our nervous system when triggered, those of us anxiously attached have an even harder time taking healthy criticism. Most often than not, we take it as a personal attack and get defensive, shut down, or redirect blame. With anxious attachment, one of our primary needs is constant reassurance from our partner that we are loved and cared for. If our significant other fails to provide this reassurance, criticizes us, or calls us out on our negative behavior, we label ourselves inadequate and unworthy of love. There could be several reasons behind this, from being criticized as children to not internalizing our achievements. The fact that we learned to overly rely on someone else for approval led to a lack of self-validation. That's why our feelings and personal security are not adequately anchored in ourselves, and we allow others' opinions to become our primary concern.

Feeling the need to control the partner, manipulate, or gaslight. Being in control of our life is a core need we all embrace and work towards. But for those with anxious attachment, the need to control everything can become consuming. Not to mention that controlling our partner can give us a sense of false relational safety. Controlling behaviors happen for various reasons in several ways. These include insisting on having things done our way, needing to be the center of attention when dysregulated, refusing to share the blame, or wanting to dictate what happens in our relationship or how our partner behaves. If we grew up in an unpredictable environment with unstable family dynamics, we developed several coping mechanisms to predict what would happen next. In adult relationships, this manifests through micromanaging our partner's life, manipulating the outcome of certain situations, gaslighting our partner, or even shifting the blame on them.

Assuming instead of asking. If we grew up witnessing dysfunctional communication techniques as children, we might have difficulties with direct communication in our adult relationships. Additionally, we are hypervigilant about our partner's mood changes and preoccupied with our own anxious thoughts. This often results in catastrophizing. Catastrophizing means we fixate on a situation's worst possible outcome and treat it as likely to happen, even when it's not. This is very common for the anxiously attached and happens in several ways through our relationships, down to the most innocent scenarios. We notice our partner's mood change and instantly assume that it's a reflection on our relationship, or we catch them in innocent flirtations and jump to the conclusion that they are having an affair. Catastrophizing thoughts fill our minds with unnecessary emotions that distract us from reality, not to mention they create false predictions in our relationships that can potentially create further rifts with our partner.

48
How does our anxious attachment get activated?

When an anxiously attached person feels something wrong in their relationship, their attachment system activates. **This attachment system is our brain's ability to monitor the safety of our relationship and the availability of our attachment figure, aka our romantic partner.** When we pick up on a threat or perceived threat to our relationship, like our partner's change of mood or behavior, our activating strategy kicks in, hijacking the brain's capacity to function normally. Our primary concern is the need to reconnect with our attachment figure. Once our attachment system is activated, we lose our ability to function normally until we manage to restore the connection with our partner. We can revert to our routines and behaviors when the connection is re-established.

When our attachment system is activated, we become consumed

with thoughts about our partner, putting them on a pedestal, recognizing only their outstanding qualities, believing this is our only chance at love, or thinking our partner is the one. This clouds our judgment completely, to the point where the anxious feeling only goes away if we get in touch with the partner and re-establish safety in the relationship. If the connection is restored and we receive reassurance in the relationship, we calm down, and everything goes back to normal. However, if our attachment needs – the need to be safe, heard, loved, and understood in our relationship – remain unmet, our protest behaviors kick in. A protest behavior is any action aimed at reestablishing the connection with our significant other and getting their attention. Common protest behaviors include:

➤ The excessive need to connect: phone calls and text messages
➤ Withdrawing: ignoring calls, avoiding conversations, stonewalling
➤ Acting hostile: eye-rolling, leaving the room, slamming doors
➤ Manipulation and playing games
➤ Trying to make the partner jealous: talking about an ex, making plans with friends, posting on social media
➤ Empty threats: threatening to leave the relationship, with no intention to follow through
➤ Keeping score: bringing up something our partner did in the past just to get even
➤ Shaming or blaming: shifting the blame and shaming our partner for something that we did

49
How to keep our activating strategies in check?

It is almost impossible to avoid being triggered in a relationship, so that should not be the goal. Neither should looking for partners who will not trigger us, as we will always be triggered in a relationship simply because it often reenacts our earliest childhood dynamics, some of which were incredibly painful. Instead, as a first step towards anxious attachment healing, we should practice self-awareness and learn to recognize our triggers and how and when we get activated. Self-awareness teaches us to pay more attention to our needs and raw parts, which we must set boundaries around. We should acknowledge our relationship needs without shame or judgment and remember we are only needy if we have unmet needs.

We need to establish a safe connection within ourselves to prevent getting activated. It means reparenting ourselves, sitting down with our unmet needs and core wounds, and establishing safety in our bodies. Instead of outsourcing our emotional validation, let's try and look for that security within and learn to give ourselves the love and reassurance we so desperately need from others.

50
What is self-regulation?

The essence of self-regulation lies in our ability to control our emotions and actions in response to them, considering what is appropriate for the situation at hand. The ability to successfully self-regulate is vital in forming, navigating, and maintaining healthy relationships. It contributes to forming healthy relational habits, including problem-solving, de-escalating conflict, and reconnecting with our partner. Not many people know that our ability to control our emotions and how we respond to them is hugely influenced by our attachment style. Therefore, while it's crucial to understand when to trust our emotions, knowing when our attachment style affects how we self-regulate is equally important.

In short, self-regulation is soothing ourselves when we feel a trigger coming up. It is managing anger, keeping our emotions in check, and reflecting before speaking. It is being aware of our activating strategies and protest behaviors.

- ➢ Self-regulation is telling our partner about our needs in a calm and collected manner.
- ➢ Self-regulation is choosing to go for a walk instead of

engaging in a pointless fight.

➤ Self-regulation is stopping ourselves from doom scrolling on social media or stalking our partner's social profiles.

➤ Self-regulation is taking ourselves out of our anxious ruminating by meditating for ten minutes.

The process and method of self-regulation are different for all of us and are deeply personal. It is based on our temperament, life choices, and often on our attachment patterns, so the best way to learn what fits us the most is to try different techniques.

51
What are your recurring patterns?

With anxious attachment, reviewing how it all started, how our core wound was created, and how we carried this wound through our adult relationships is helpful. We all have recurring patterns that relate to our attachment style, indicating attachment wounds throughout our entire dating history. That's why it's vital to take a moment and review what is the recurring theme we carry from partnership to partnership. This could be anything from being clingy, habitually overstepping our partner's boundaries, being fixated on the speed with which our partner responds to our texts, never saying no, or acting out of jealousy.

In essence, a relationship pattern is repeating the same behaviors over and over again with new people in our life. We can exhibit these patterns in romantic relationships, friendships, and work relationships. They indicate three main things:

➤ **Who do we get into relationships with**, do we choose the same type of person, and if so, why

➤ **Our interactions with them**, the behaviors we exhibit around them while in the relationship, common protest behaviors, communication techniques, expression of needs, and boundaries

➢ **How we let them treat us**, what do we allow them to do, and how do we allow these people to treat us in the partnership

To identify your recurring patterns try to work backward and examine your current or past relationships. Examine your role in the dynamic and your partner's role. Is there a recurring theme? Do you keep repeating the same behavior? Do you recognize the same scenarios or relational dynamic play out in each instance with a different partner? Work to identify the most common recurring patterns in your current and past relationships. This can help you prevent repeating them and going through the same pain and heartbreak in every new relationship.

Relationship patterns can look like this:

➢ "I feel intense anxiety when my partner wants to take time away from our relationship."
➢ "Every time I get upset over something, I rehearse speeches in my head repeatedly, but never share it with my partner."
➢ "I purposefully create problems in my relationship because resolving them brings me closer to my partner."
➢ "I keep choosing people who are emotionally unavailable."
➢ "If I feel emotional distance from my partner, I become unsure of my value and project my insecurities on my partner by picking fights."
➢ "I am scared that my partner will leave me, so I encourage them to put themselves first in the partnership while I neglect myself."

52
The relationship role archetypes

To help you identify the recurring patterns in your relationship, here are the three main archetypes that anxiously attached people might fall into

The caretaker. In this mothering role, we care for our partner's every need, allowing them to lean comfortably into the relationship. We clean the house, prepare the meals, take care of the children, allowing our significant other to enjoy their lives, taking over all the responsibilities from them. This eventually builds up resentment and leads to conflict.

With this role, we pick partners who need saving or fixing, people who need taking care of, and play into the role. We think, "If I could get them to do (your choice of change), they would be so much better off." or "If I did (your choice of service) for them, their life and relationship with me would change/improve/shift, etc."

Needless to say, this role doesn't consider our partner, their needs, or desires. It is all about creating safety in our relationship by trying to control our partner's life, the outcome of certain situations, or how other people view us as partners.

The leader. This role is the opposite of the caretaker, and it indicates that we want to be in charge all the time. This concerns us being the primary decision-maker, the driving force behind the relationship. We set the tone, and our partner mainly plays by our rules.

This role can look like always initiating contact, planning the dates, or being the one to suggest important relationship milestones, like moving in together. This can turn into extremes, where we push in on our partner's private times, become demanding, or expect them to keep us updated on everything that happens in their lives. This role is again more about control than helping out someone who is 'indecisive.' If we can keep tabs on the relationship, then we feel safe. If we control our partner's life, we will be less likely to be abandoned because we made ourselves worthwhile.

The codependent. This relationship dynamic happens when one or both partners become overly dependent on the other. It is prevalent if either partner gets prematurely attached to the other or if they become a unit too soon, giving up their individual lives and hobbies and neglecting their friendships or family. The codependent role is typical with anxious-anxious partners, where both partners struggle to form an interdependent relationship. This role can be harmful, and it has the potential to doom the partnership before it even has a chance to begin.

It is important to note that our partner isn't and shouldn't be our primary or only source of contact, support, validation, or reassurance. We need to establish a healthy network and support system outside the relationship. This will, on the one hand, take the edge off of our partner to meet our needs and, on the other hand, can support us should we face relational challenges.

53
Is it you, or is it your partner?

We need to be able to distinguish between our own patterns that stem from our attachment styles and the behavior that warrants us getting triggered. While dating or being in a relationship with other people, we encounter a lot of different dynamics. Some people are unfaithful, and some habitually avoid being in a committed relationship. Some people open the dating phase with intense love-bombing just to drop everything a few months later, and some have deep-rooted insecurities that make them lash out at us whenever we make them uncomfortable.

It's essential to be aware of what recurring issues are caused by our own attachment and what is a reasonable reaction to our partner's behavior. Try to work it out by going over your past relationships. Make a list of past issues and triggers if needed, then identify the recurring problems that are a direct impact of your anxious attachment. Revisiting past pain and traumas can be incredibly difficult for some, but it is helpful to gain clarity on our anxiously attached behavior is beneficial. Remember, don't shame or blame yourself for whatever may come up. Practice self-compassion and try to look at your past patterns objectively.

54
What emotions come up when you're triggered?

Practice noticing the feelings behind your trigger reactions. Emotional literacy takes us one step closer to understanding ourselves. It also makes it easier to express these feelings to our partners. The primary benefit, however, is understanding that emotions have a way of triggering survival behaviors in us. Human emotions have developed through evolution as a survival mechanism, and when we understand what they're trying to signal, we can address the real need under the surface. If we don't, we keep reliving our negative stories attached to the core beliefs we formed as children. This results in repeating the same relational patterns, feeling the same feelings, and thinking the same thoughts without questioning their validity.

An example of unconscious pattern repetition:

➤ A triggering event happens to us
➤ This triggers an internalized issue: unresolved past patterns, insecurities, fear, anxiety, core wounds, etc.
➤ As a response, we unconsciously create a story around this event and make assumptions as to why this is happening
➤ These assumptions now influence our reactions, feelings, and thoughts
➤ We act out on these thoughts, and unconsciously reinforce them through our negative thought patterns
➤ The core belief is now reinforced proving to us the negative meaning we attached to the original story

This happens because our brain has a way to protect us by creating negative stories and attaching negative meanings to events. The brain considers uncertainty dangerous and a threat, so a negative story feels like a much safer choice. This practice of creating self-fulfilling prophecies prevents us from getting hurt or exposing ourselves to further danger.

55
Using our emotions to cultivate a better understanding

Our feelings aren't just reactions. They are our brain's way of making sense of the information and physical sensations around us. We can start using emotions to understand ourselves better when we realize this. **We benefit in many ways by developing the ability to understand and express our emotions. We can manage stress better, communicate with others, and develop self-compassion.** We should not suppress our feelings; instead, we should use them as pointers to discover our core needs and values.

An easy exercise to deepen our self-awareness is noticing and labeling our emotions. When we label emotions as we experience them, we create distance between them and our reactions. By simply saying 'I feel __,' we can keep our reaction under control and move on quicker. The more we practice labeling our feelings, the better we become at understanding our inner world.

We can use our emotions as tools of self-regulation. When we understand and can name our emotions, we can respond to them and communicate them better. It also helps us understand our partner's moods better.

56
What is a core wound?

A core wound is something that many of us carry with us throughout our lives. **It's an emotional wound that we form from suppressed pain that we experienced in childhood.** These wounds can be challenging to heal, but it's essential to recognize them and work through them to move forward and live a fulfilling life. Whether through therapy, self-reflection, or other methods, addressing our core wounds can help us break free from negative patterns and live more authentically. Core wounds can be the byproduct of abandonment, bullying, neglect, inconsistencies, invalidation, gaslighting, or abuse.

Core wounds run deep and get triggered by adult experiences, primarily relational experiences. They defy intellect, so while our thinking brains are aware of our worth and we know that we feel disproportionate about these, we still can't help them. When core wounds are triggered, they have a physical manifestation in our bodies, with people reporting feeling dizziness, heart racing, the feeling of air sucked out of their lungs, drowning, and even panic. Let's have a look at the most relevant core wounding with anxious attachment.

The rejection core wound develops from instances when our parent pushes away or ignores us. This might mean that we are actively dating people who end up ghosting us or ditching abruptly with no warning. This core wound results in **the need for attention, the need to be seen and heard**. It can cause us to become clingy and needy of our partner, sometimes demanding.

With this core wound, we feel that we are not enough, we do not count, or we are overlooked; even in a loving relationship and with a supportive partner, this core wound gets triggered every time we feel overlooked, ignored, or not chosen.

Our internalized beliefs are:

- ➤ "I am not important, I am constantly overlooked"
- ➤ "I have no value, I am not a good person"
- ➤ "I am not desired, no one will ever want me"

The abandonment wound develops if your parent was inconsistent, unpredictable or absent. This might mean that in your adult relationships, you choose people who make you constantly worry that they will abandon you too. The abandonment wound results in the **need for affection, a need to connect to someone else, to belong, and create a connection**. This is often why we attach prematurely to partners, put them on a pedestal, and refuse to see their red flags until too late. We desperately need to be chosen by our person. We feel that we are not connected; we are not loved.

Our internalized beliefs are:

> - "I am all alone"
> - "No one understands or cares"
> - "They will leave me, as they always do"
> - "I need to do more, or I will be abandoned"

The enmeshment core wound develops when the boundaries between the child and parent are blurred, or simply nonexistent. This might contribute to you ending up in relationships where your identity is completely absorbed into your partner's, where you constantly cater to their needs, losing your sense of personality and neglecting your own needs. It results in a sense of timidness in relationships, starting to act, react, feel, and behave like the partner. With this wound, there is a need to feel accepted, be similar to, or want similar things to the partner.

Our internalized beliefs are:

> - "I need to fit in to be accepted"
> - "There should be no secrets between partners"
> - "I must do everything in my power to please my partner because that's normal"

The shame core wound develops when you grow up facing constant shaming or criticism from a caregiver. You may internalize this as you are inherently bad or flawed. This shows up in your adult relationships by mainly opting for partners who reinforce this belief system, helping it to set in even more. It's a catch-22 where your partners will continually reaffirm this core belief, pushing you further into believing that something is wrong with you, so you keep choosing partners who reaffirm this, helping the negative belief set in even further.

Our internalized beliefs are:

➤ "I'm not good enough to deserve a better life, relationship"
➤ "I can never get anything right; I'm not enough to make a relationship work."
➤ "I can't show up as my true self because it's flawed, and if my partner recognizes it, he will leave."

The helplessness core wound develops when we are left to fend for ourselves, as our caregiver isn't available to tend to our immediate needs. When we needed help, soothing, or reassurance as children, nobody was coming to our aid, and we felt powerless. This core wound results in a deep need for approval, often paired with self-hatred. This wound makes us feel like we are not good enough, are not competent, will never achieve our goals, or are a failure. Someone with this core wound may need a lot of reassurance and may outsource all the validation for their decisions or life choices to their friends, family members, or romantic partners.

Our internalized beliefs are:

➤ "I don't know what to do, I don't feel confident to decide"
➤ "I can't change it, I simply don't have the power to turn that situation around"
➤ "I am a failure, I'm simply inadequate in everything I do"

Parentification happens when a child is made to feel responsible for the emotional or physical needs of their parent or caregiver. This can lead to wanting to save, fix or caretake partners in our adult relationships, neglecting our wellbeing. This happens because we unconsciously feel the need to replicate and resolve our past issues.

The roles of fixer, savior, and caretaker are typical manifestations of the parentification wound but are mainly aimed at trying to control the outcome of certain situations to feel safe in the relationship.

Our internalized beliefs are:

> ➢ "My only worth comes from caring for people."
> ➢ "I need to help my partner so that they can be content and whole."
> ➢ "My value is helping others to change and improve themselves."

The mistrust wound develops when the caregiver is abusive or neglectful towards the child, leading to feelings of skepticism and suspicion in adult relationships. With this core wound, you might end up dating people who prove this distrust well-founded, creating a self-fulfilling prophecy and solidifying this belief system.

Our internalized beliefs are:

> ➢ "People are unpredictable and will only end up hurting me."
> ➢ "I am better off alone. No one can be trusted.'

57
Can you identify your core wounds?

Core wounds can lead to various issues, including reactions that can negatively impact our lives or compensating behaviors like emotional eating, stress, anxiety, panic, or even self-harm. But most importantly, when triggered, our core wound can cause disconnection with ourselves and others. Below is a list of some of the most common core wounds connected to anxious attachment. Can you identify any of them?

> **Feeling imperfect**

We compensate by trying to prove our worth, seeking internal and external perfection by trying to control or perfect ourselves and others. There is a tendency here to show ourselves in a better light, and we often end up flaunting or bragging, as well as highlighting or exaggerating our positive side.

> **Feeling worthless**

We compensate by fixing, saving, or caretaking other people, often overstepping our boundaries and neglecting our needs in the process. With this core wound, we struggle with codependency and can come across as overly clingy or needy, craving constant validation and reassurance from our partner.

> **Feeling alone**

We compensate by attaching prematurely to our partners, seeking connection through our romantic relationships, and over-connecting to people. This gives us a constant high as we believe that connection will heal us; in the meantime, we fail to nurture the most important relationship, the one with ourselves.

> **Feeling incomplete**

We compensate by looking for the perfect partner to complete us. We project a huge fantasy on most of our dates, putting them on a pedestal. At the same time, we neglect to deepen the connection and get to know our person well. Instead, we live in a fantasy where we are a couple now, are whole, and complete each other.

➤ Feeling powerless

We compensate by showing up overly powerful, tapping into our masculine energies, and imagining ourselves just a little more than we actually are. This is usually overpowering for any romantic partner and can confuse many.

➤ Feeling loveless

We compensate by appearing overly loving and caring; however, deep down, we have an almost impenetrable passive-aggressive core that causes a lot of repressed anger. There is pretty much nothing beyond the loving core, as deep down, we aren't ready to receive love.

58
The abandonment wound

Anxious attachment is centered around an intense fear of rejection and abandonment. **Those of us suffering from abandonment wounds are extremely sensitive to cues of rejection**, for example, feeling insignificant, criticized, misunderstood, excluded, or overlooked.

With abandonment wounds, we may have consistent relationship challenges, especially in romantic partnerships. This includes being afraid of conflict, rejection, or being unwanted; because of this, we people-please and self-abandon as a survival strategy.

When our attachment system gets activated, we can't think clearly. Our painful emotions flood our system and distort our perception of reality. **That is when the old narratives start playing out, influencing how we act, react, think, feel, and behave.** This might resurface in crying, screaming, panicking, and all these reactions feel very childlike. When our abandonment wound is triggered, we automatically default to the meanings we created of the world around us when we were little.

Abandonment wounds are often created by an absent parent figure, emotionally unavailable parents, being given the silent treatment, or being yelled at or punished for no reason. **With this core wound, we firmly believe that love is conditional, and we must work hard to be loved and cared for.** We don't feel good enough, and we think we need to work extra hard because that is the story we created in childhood. It is almost like we were unconsciously conditioned to perform for love in several ways:

- If I get good grades, my parents will like me more.
- If I behave well, my mom will let me go to the playground with my friends
- If I don't bother my dad and stay silent, he will take me with him to watch the game

Common consequences of the abandonment wound are workaholism, over-eating, being a high-achiever, hiding certain 'undesirable' aspects of our personalities, people-pleasing, and becoming chameleons who mold their ways to their partner's needs.

59
Self-fulfilling prophecies

Self-fulfilling prophecies are connected to our core wounds and are not exclusive to anxiously attached people; we are all guilty of them. **A self-fulfilling prophecy is an unfounded or false thought that leads to its confirmation.** In other words, our expectations of a person or situation will eventually result in them confirming our thoughts. It is a powerful phenomenon we should all be aware of. It works using our confirmation bias by validating our internalized ideas on a subject.

For example, the anxious-preoccupied person has a deep-rooted belief that they are not good enough and that their partner will eventually abandon them. This belief makes them act out in controlling, manipulative ways or prompts them to become hypervigilant. This might get their partner fed up and end the relationship, confirming their original belief and fulfilling their prophecy. Ironically, it might not even occur to them that they were the engineer of their own failure.

How to start working on yourself?

60
The anxiously attached healing journey

The anxiously attached healing journey looks a lot like a thorough self-evaluation, followed by a plan that we consistently follow through. Think of it like setting up a solid blueprint. You work out who you are, what triggers you, and what patterns you repeat unconsciously, then map out how to replace your anxious habits with secure ones. You will practice taking yourself out of triggering situations, self-soothing, reflecting, and returning to the problem with clear, honest communication, clarity, and empathy. Starting your healing journey can be confusing and overwhelming, but it'll get easier as you become familiar with what inner work means. In the next chapters, I will walk you through a series of questions and exercises that will help you start working on yourself by yourself. You can do these at your own speed, don't feel you have to rush anything. We all heal at our own pace.

61
Secure attachment

The goal of anxious attachment healing is to develop an earned secure attachment, so let's look at what that looks like in a relationship. The most common type of attachment in Western society is secure attachment, with – according to research – approximately 66% of the US population securely attached. It is the healthiest form of attachment. It's based on parental best practices that make the child feel comforted by their parent, who is attuned to their needs. Securely attached children feel protected by their caregiver, believing they have someone they can rely on. These children can seek comfort in their caregiver and are comfortable exploring their surroundings in the presence of the parent figure. Secure attachment is crucial to healthy development because it impacts an individual's emotional life and, by extension, adult relationships.

Growing up experiencing a sense of stability around them, securely attached children find it easier to interact with the world around them. They are more open and accepting of the ideas and opinions of others and are flexible in exploring unknown territories, whether it's physical or emotional.

Adults with secure attachment report having higher self-esteem and healthier long-term relationships. Since they grow up modeling a positive caregiver relationship, securely attached people can create a healthy connection with others in all areas of their lives. Securely attached people are more social, warm, and easy to connect to. They are in touch with and can express their feelings. They can build deep, meaningful, and long-lasting relationships with others.

Securely attached people:

- ➢ Can plan and think of long-term goals with their partner
- ➢ Can regulate emotions and feelings in a relationship
- ➢ Are great at bonding, opening up to, & trusting others
- ➢ Are selfless, generous, and trusting with their partner
- ➢ Are willing to offer an apology or resolution to problems when needed
- ➢ Are comfortable being alone or give their partner time alone when needed
- ➢ Actively seek emotional support from their partner and also provide emotional support in return
- ➢ Are comfortable with closeness & mutual dependency
- ➢ Can set and respect healthy and flexible boundaries
- ➢ Can communicate needs effectively
- ➢ Have the assertiveness to seek out healthy relational habits

and build upon them

➤ Can walk away from people or situations that don't match their needs, long-term goals, or expectations

➤ Do see themselves and others in a positive light, assume the best of others

➤ Proactively seek support from their partners, or loved ones, without becoming overly dependent on anybody

➤ Can let others in, actively listening to them and offering support without fixing or caretaking

➤ Are confident and decisive in their partnerships and life in general

62
Self-love

The concept of self-love can be fleeting for most of us. We think, 'Oh, but I like myself,' while we have a variety of ways we betray our trust, sabotage our relationships and overstep our boundaries. In essence, self-love means high regard for our well-being and happiness. It means taking care of our needs and not sacrificing ourselves to please others. Self-love means not settling for less than we deserve, prioritizing and trusting ourselves, talking about ourselves positively, setting healthy boundaries, and learning to forgive our mistakes.

Ways to practice self-love include:

Becoming mindful. It translates into being able to tune into what we think and how we feel at the present moment without giving in to any interruptions around us. It is shown to have many benefits, from balancing our mood to reducing stress levels.

Practicing self-care. It is proven that people who take better care of themselves report higher overall satisfaction in their lives and relationships. Good self-care habits include healthy nutrition, regular physical exercise, healthy social life, and proper sleep.

Opting for healthy choices. By opting for healthy choices, you encourage yourself to value your needs and start looking at yourself as a high-value person. This can be anything from choosing a healthy home-cooked meal over takeout to saying no to inconsistent dating patterns.

Learning to say 'no'. With anxious attachment, we dismiss our feelings, minimize our problems, and neglect to express our needs out of fear of coming across as needy or high-maintenance. So learning to say 'no' to things we don't want to allow into our lives or that we don't have the emotional or mental capacity for will be a crucial part of the healing process. This might sound overwhelming initially, but cognitive behavioral therapy tells us that if we fear something and expose ourselves to it repeatedly, we will gradually learn that nothing terrible will happen to us. Moreover, we'll eventually see the situation as safe and become desensitized to the threat.

So if saying 'no' feels threatening, try taking baby steps by drawing healthy boundaries around the request.

> ➤ "I would love to help you with this, but I don't have the time this week. If that works for you, I can manage a few hours next week."
> ➤ "I would love to join you and your friends, but I won't be able to stay very long."
> ➤ "I am not comfortable spending a whole weekend with your family. Could we work out something else instead? Perhaps a family dinner next week?"
> ➤ "I don't have the emotional capacity to discuss this now, but I would love to help you out some other way."

Getting into the practice of meeting our own needs. Meeting our needs sounds profound, yet many of us dismiss our own needs and wants 'in the interest of the relationship.' So a great way to shift this in the right direction is to ask yourself, "What do I need right now? What could I do for myself or give myself to feel better in this situation?" And the answer might be much easier than you think. It could be some time alone, a nice bubble bath, a healthy home-cooked meal, or regular yoga or fitness classes. Paying attention to our bodies and relearning to be in tune with ourselves will tremendously impact our lives and partnerships.

Purging toxic relationships and behavior from our life. Work to reduce the times you are subjected to anything that triggers you or sends your nervous system into fight or flight mode. The easiest way to achieve this in your romantic life is to date securely attached people; however, this isn't always possible. So work to reduce the times you get triggered by recognizing what triggers you and laying clear and firm boundaries around this behavior. Let your partner know what is and isn't acceptable and what you need to stay safe and reassured in the relationship. Also, pay attention to your reactions in triggering situations and learn to recognize them when they happen so that you can leave and self-regulate. Work to limit your time around people or situations that trigger you. For example, if you find your partner's friends or family upsetting, limit your contact or time with them. Putting your own mental health and well-being might feel selfish at first, especially if you are used to sacrificing your own needs in the interest of others, so again, take baby steps.

63
Improving your self-esteem

Self-esteem shows how much we evaluate ourselves positively; it represents how much we love and value ourselves. Self-esteem revolves around our opinion of ourselves and how we learn to value ourselves, our efforts, our looks, and good or bad traits. There's a difference between self-esteem and self-confidence. Self-esteem affects how we see ourselves, while self-confidence dictates how we perceive and present our skills and talents.

Much of having healthy self-esteem has to do with upbringing, as this is also influenced by our childhood experiences. It is up to parents to teach their children healthy self-belief and self-confidence, and if we learn this in childhood, we will be more confident and competent in everything we do. When our parents do not teach us these, they allow us to internalize our mistakes and wallow in our failures. With anxious attachment, if we weren't taught to have proper self-belief and self-confidence, then we outsource validation and reassurance to those closest to us and lower our own self-esteem. We become unsure about our choices, thoughts, and even decisions, to the point where we constantly seek reassurance and fail to think highly of ourselves, constantly comparing ourselves to others.

With low self-esteem, our mental health can suffer, not to mention our relationships, as we tend to seek validation from people around us. If we have low self-esteem, we tend to be very critical of ourselves and tend to isolate ourselves more. It can also hinder our efforts to develop a growth mindset.

Working to improve your self-esteem will help you establish safety within. This means you won't have to turn to someone else for validation or reassurance because you can be more self-reliant in meeting your needs. To raise your self-esteem, the first step is to pay attention to how you speak to yourself, spot negative self-talk, and replace it with a positive, reaffirming one.

Steps to achieve higher self-esteem:

- ➤ **Boost your sense of accomplishment** by doing something that makes you feel rewarded and successful, no matter what.
- ➤ **Step out of your comfort zone.** It doesn't have to be something big; taking a different route to work or trying a new activity will do the trick. The point here is that when you succeed in your new endeavors, you teach yourself that you can persevere through tough times and are more resilient

than you think.

➢ **Notice when you get something right** and pat yourself on the shoulder. This will work as a positive reinforcement making it easier to achieve anything the next time.

➢ **Don't beat yourself up** for your mistakes. Let go of self-shaming or blame. Instead, learn to be more compassionate with yourself and strive to do better the next time around.

➢ **Do things that make you feel alive**, even if it's a small thing. Switch up your daily routine, start a new hobby, or learn a language. This will give you an immense sense of accomplishment and reward.

➢ **Stop comparing yourself to others.** Remember, your progress, physical beauty, or worthiness should never be determined by how well others are doing or how beautiful they appear to be. You are on your unique journey and should focus on growth and development. Comparing yourself to others will only lead to unnecessary stress and negative emotions. Instead, celebrate your successes and appreciate the beauty within yourself. Staying off social media can help a lot; if it's not an option, keep reminding yourself that people only share the best, most flattening moments on their social profiles.

➢ **Celebrate your wins.** Achievements come in all different shapes and sizes. If you managed to get to yoga class today or cleaned up the bathroom, that's already cause for celebration. Celebrating even small achievements is essential because they require effort and contribute to your growth and development. Keep shifting your focus towards noticing your accomplishments, no matter how big or small, and give yourself the praise you deserve.

➢ **Let go of negative people.** The people you surround yourself with have a massive impact on your mood and level of self-esteem. Surrounding yourself with people constantly reminding you of your flaws and filling you with self-doubt will harm your mental health. And while it's often not possible to cut them out completely, try to set firm boundaries around how they talk to you or limit your interactions with them.

➤ **Speak up for yourself.** It's essential to speak up and make yourself heard if you want to achieve your goals and get what you want in life. Feel free to ask for what you need, whether at work, in relationships, or in other areas of your life. By communicating your needs clearly and confidently, you can create better opportunities to achieve your goals and meet your needs. Remember, no one can read your mind, so if you want something, you must ask for it!

64
Validate your thoughts and feelings

Everyone needs validation, the feeling of being accepted and understood. However, anxiously attached people seek external validation at an unhealthy level. We rely on others to make us feel good, doubt our abilities, and obsessively check in with friends or partners looking for approval. At the same time, we question our worth if others don't reflect it to us. Relying on external validation can make us more anxious, making disapproval and criticism even more painful because we put so much value on others' opinions.

When we rely on others to make us feel good, we allow them to dictate our worth and begin to distrust our thoughts, feelings, and judgments. Consequently, we become needy and ask for validation in ways that may turn our partners off. External validation can be great but should only come after self-validation. So how do we validate ourselves? By encouraging ourselves, prioritizing our needs, treating ourselves with understanding and kindness, and accepting our flaws and mistakes. Here are a few great affirmations to help you practice self-validation.

My needs matter too	It's ok to be upset over this
My feelings are important even if my partner cannot validate them	I'm making progress here, even if it is slow
I am worthy	I'm not perfect, and it's ok
It's okay to get positive reassurance from my partner	Wanting an explanation doesn't make me needy
I will take time to celebrate my success	I am the best judge of what is good for me and what isn't
I prioritize my mental health, and so I step away from this argument	I don't need to prove my worth to anyone
It's okay to cry, or take time out when I feel low	This is hard. How could I make this a little easier on me?
It didn't turn out how I intended, but I gave it my best effort	Not everyone likes me, and that is okay. I like myself, and it's perfectly enough
Even though I'm anxiously attached, the problem isn't always me	I overreacted, but I will go back and apologize once I am calm and collected

65
Don't over-explain

Anxiously attached people often show their need to be accepted and loved by overexplaining their choices, decisions, or even themselves. I'm sure you've been there too! You started dating someone new and felt such an incredible connection with them that you felt justified to share more than necessary. Or perhaps you declined an invitation but felt so guilty that you kept going on and on, explaining why you couldn't make it.

Communicating and being vulnerable with the right people is great, but over-explaining your life choices or decisions is unnecessary. **We over-explain when we don't feel comfortable or justified to make a decision or have learned to outsource our validation to people around us.** But in reality, as long as you know what's right for you, you don't have to share your reasons or have anyone else approve of your decisions, not even those closest to you. Work to validate your choices, decisions, and feelings without anyone else having a say in them. This will contribute to a more healthy, fulfilled, and interdependent relationship.

66
Shift your perspective

Following through with a change often comes down to challenging ourselves and, shifting our perspective, rethinking our small daily habits. It is no different for anxiously attached people. So if you find it overwhelming to get started with the work, here are several small steps you can take to rewire your way of thinking to develop more secure habits.

Try to find happiness in the small things around you. These could be anything from laughing with friends to reading a great book or having your favorite takeaway coffee, or walking in the park. This might sound simple, but you don't need to seek happiness outside of you when it's all around.

Connect with people around you on a different level, so you don't have to rely on one person as a source of love and fulfillment. We are social beings, and seeking the company of others is part of our well-being. So surround yourself with friends, colleagues, and workout buddies and learn to cultivate a great relationship with them. This will add more satisfaction to your daily life and help you form an interdependent relationship with your partner.

Find fulfillment in solo activities. Go to the gym, sign up for a book club, volunteer, or go to church. Being alone while doing something meaningful will give you a sense of achievement and teach you to appreciate your own company. Doing this will contribute to a more secure self and help you develop your independence quicker.

Think of your relationship differently. We grew up with an idealized version of what love is. We believe in 'the one' and 'happily ever after,' and while these notions sound beautiful, they don't reflect reality. So try to shift your perspective. Question the fairytale ideas, and think about what a relationship really means to you. What I find a healthy way to think about it is a relationship is a safe space for two people to come together, heal, and grow. It's not a forever thing; it's not always a happy thing; it's not always smooth sailing.

So question what you think about the following aspects; time spent together, communicating needs, conflict, and resolution, having different needs, having other friend groups, mistakes and mess ups, future plans, value systems, building the relationship after the honeymoon phase is over, what if you guys grow apart, moving together, distributing chores, paying bills, financial responsibility, children or no children. Considering these will help ease the human aspect into your romance and take some pressure off your partner and yourself.

67
Self-regulation and self-awareness

These are robust tools we need to learn to start reparenting ourselves. Self-awareness is our ability to notice how our actions, thoughts, or emotions do or don't align with our inner self. If we are self-aware, we can objectively evaluate ourselves align our behavior with our values, and understand how others perceive us. In comparison, self-regulation is the ability to control our emotions and the actions we take in response to them, considering what is appropriate for each situation. The ability to self-regulate is vital in successfully creating and maintaining healthy relationships. Not many people know that our ability to control our emotions and how we respond to them is influenced by our attachment style. And while, while it's important to understand when to trust our emotions, it's equally important to know how our attachment style impacts how we self-regulate. Self-regulation is learned in early childhood through our primary caregivers, who teach us how to downregulate negative and upregulate positive emotions. If co-regulation doesn't happen, we must learn emotional grounding techniques to regulate our nervous system in our adult years.

68
Emotional grounding techniques

Emotional grounding techniques are widely recommended by therapists and coaches to help their clients navigate dissociation or overwhelm. When a strong reaction kicks in, we can start spacing out, leaving our bodies and getting worked up, feeling like we are not in control anymore. That's when these techniques come in handy because they can help pull us away from flashbacks, unwanted memories, or negative emotions. Grounding techniques help us refocus on the present moment and distract ourselves from our anxious thoughts and feelings. There are several methods, from journaling, yoga, EFT tapping, belly breathing, and meditation to simply putting your hands under cold water. In the following chapters, I will go through the most effective exercises.

Journaling

You might remember keeping a diary from your teenage years, a place to jot down your struggles and fears without judgment. The concept and benefits of journaling as an adult are the same. By writing down your thoughts and feelings, you achieve clarity and create distance between intrusive thoughts and reality. And if you struggle with stress, depression, or anxiety, keeping a journal can be a great idea. It can help you gain control of your emotions and improve your mental health.

Journaling can help you control your moods, manage your anxiety and even cope with depression. It lets you see your problems more clearly and helps identify negative thoughts or behaviors. If you are anxiously attached, it can be a fantastic tool to write down your anxious 'episodes' whenever you get triggered, overreact or go into a fit of rage. It's also great to write about what is going through your head when you get triggered in an honest and non-judgemental way. This practice can help you identify your patterns later and understand what triggers you the most.

EFT tapping

Another fantastic technique to unlearn our subconscious negative beliefs is EFT tapping. The emotional freedom technique is an alternative treatment to ease emotional distress in anxiety, depression, or PTSD. This technique harnesses the body's energy system by tapping the main meridian points.

According to its developer, Gary Craig, an energy disruption is the cause of all negative emotions and pain. Though still being researched, EFT tapping has been used to treat people with several anxiety-related issues. The emotional freedom technique is believed to be a very effective way to free negative energies, thoughts, and feelings stored in our bodies. It uses a unique method to tap on the main energy points while repeating limiting beliefs, effectively releasing them.

The steps to EFT tapping:

➢ Identify the issue. Focusing on one problem at a time is believed to be most effective.
➢ Determine how painful the problem is on a scale of 1 to 10. This will help you after each session when you check back on how strongly you feel about the issue when the session is complete.

➤ Set it up. You usually begin by acknowledging the problem, then forgiving yourself. A common phrase is: "Even though I have low self-worth, I love and accept myself," "Even though I act out when triggered, I am worthy and lovable."

➤ The sequence of tapping: top of the head – between the eyebrows – on the temple – under the eyes – under the nose – on the chin – at the beginning of the collarbone – top of the head. You can tap just one side of your face or both, whatever you feel most comfortable with. How you set the pressure is up to you how you set the pressure, but light tapping is recommended.

➤ Continue tapping for as long as you feel a release of the negative emotion. Test the initial feeling's intensity; how strong do you feel about it now on a scale of 1 to 10?

Visualizing

People have been using several visualization exercises for centuries; however, it often gets a bad rep for being too holistic. But the truth is that these techniques can be highly beneficial and are used by professional athletes and CEOs. Visualization is the technique of imagining your future as if it has already happened. This practice harnesses the power of the brain that cannot tell the difference between something that has already happened and something you imagine has happened.

With anxious attachment, visualization exercises can be used as a mental rehearsal, where you imagine yourself in a triggering situation and follow a set-out process to soothe yourself, calm your nervous system, and respond from a place of security instead of fear. This exercise will help you mentally rehearse your reactions in anticipation of the triggering event so that when it actually happens, you can tap into your calm.

Other mindfulness techniques

Mindfulness is our ability to be fully present in our bodies without being overwhelmed by what's happening around us. These are some of my favorite techniques that you can use to calm yourself effectively when triggered.

Mindfulness meditation helps you learn to stay with complicated feelings without analyzing, suppressing, or encouraging them. Allowing yourself to feel and acknowledge your worries, irritations, painful memories, and other emotions often helps them deplete. It provides a safe space to explore thoughts and feelings without judgment or shame.

Try to ground yourself in the present moment for a simple exercise and listen to your breath. Bring the focus on the body and try noticing your bodily sensations without attaching meaning to them. If a thought comes up, notice it and let it pass. Stay there observing the body for as long as you can.

Positive affirmations are statements you repeat to yourself daily, grounding yourself in a new reality you create through them. They can be incredibly beneficial for anxiously attached people simply because they provide a way to rewrite subconscious negative beliefs. Try connecting them with a calming breathing exercise, and repeat them when anxiety arises. Try writing them down in a notebook if you find it difficult to say them out loud or in your head. Positive affirmations in themselves will not advance the healing process. You must do the groundwork of discovering and reframing your negative patterns, catching your negative self-talk, and reframing old, dysfunctional thought patterns before applying them successfully.

Examples of positive affirmations:

- ➤ "I am safe and protected in my body."
- ➤ "I am enough and worthy of love."
- ➤ "I release my past mistakes, and I embrace the present."
- ➤ "I can move past any triggering moment. All my feelings are temporary, and this will pass too."
- ➤ "I am loved and cared for in my relationship even when my

partner and I spend time apart."

Belly breathing, also called diaphragmatic breathing, is a breathing technique you can hugely benefit from. Its positive impacts include reducing your blood pressure and heart rate, helping you relay easier. When you breathe normally, you don't use your total lung capacity; however, with diaphragmatic breathing, you can help increase lung efficiency. It's proven to help you relax, increase the amount of oxygen in your blood, and reduce blood pressure and heart rate. It's believed to help reduce anxiety and normalize our body's response in stressful situations.

Begin by taking up a comfortable position, either sitting or lying down. Then place one hand on your chest and another below the ribcage on your belly. Then breathe in slowly through your nose so your belly moves out against your hand, but your chest remains in the same position. Then slowly tighten your stomach muscles so the air leaves your lungs, exhaling through your lips. Repeat for 5-10 minutes. With each repetition, try to increase the amount of air you breathe in.

Shaking the body can help regulate the nervous system, returning the body to rest and digest state when overstimulated. Trauma and tension-releasing exercises, like shaking, may be beneficial in managing and relieving stress. It works as the autonomic nervous system regulates our bodies through upregulation and downregulation. Upregulation increases our energy levels, while downregulation decreases it. When we experience stressors or a perceived threat, our autonomic nervous system responds by releasing adrenaline and cortisol into the bloodstream. This process increases heart rate, raising the energy levels in the body in case it needs to respond to a perceived threat. However, the body can also overreact to stressors, such as relationship problems or perceived threats in our partnerships.

This is when the process of downregulation comes in handy, bringing our nervous system back to neutral and resetting our bodily functions to normal. Shaking is an effective and fun way of doing it. Try standing or sitting down, shaking one part of your body at a time. Try shaking your hands and arms and focus on how it makes you feel. You are not looking for any specific sensation here; just focus on how it makes you feel relieved. If it feels good, continue shaking down your legs too, or rotating your upper body swinging from left to right.

Yoga. More and more people turn to yoga to reduce anxiety and balance their out-of-tune nervous system. Many find that focusing on the breath and the ability to be present in each pose can help quiet negative mental chatter and boost their overall mood. While there is not one specific exercise, according to practitioners, every pose that helps relieve tension in and around the hips is a fantastic way to soothe ourselves. So is rocking from side to side or front to back while lying on our backs.

My favorite mindfulness technique, however, is simply **noticing your surroundings**. Use all your senses to notice what's happening around you, no matter where you are. What can you see, smell, hear, taste, or touch? Make an effort to notice the little things you might not always pay attention to, like the color of the cars on the street or the noise your feet make when touching the ground. Get immersed in this exercise a little before you allow yourself to return to your thoughts.

An anchoring phrase will be helpful when you feel an overwhelming physical or mental reaction to a trigger. Anchoring phrases are used to ground yourself in the present moment, reactivating your prefrontal cortex by repeating a simple phrase. Something that you feel familiar and comfortable with. It sounds like, 'My name is Anna. I'm 36 years old. I live in London, and I am currently on my way home.' You can add to this list by noticing your surroundings and stating simple observations: 'It's sunny today; I will start preparing dinner soon.' Repeat until you feel calmer.

Paying attention to your body is a great technique, as you can do it virtually anywhere, any time. Start paying attention to your body, skin, any object you are making contact with, your internal sensations, etc.

This might look like this:

- ➤ Your hair touching your face or shoulders
- ➤ You feel hungry or thirsty
- ➤ Your legs make contact with the chair
- ➤ Your heartbeat is normal
- ➤ There is wind or rain on your face
- ➤ You feel stiffness somewhere in your body

Picking up or touching items near you and paying attention to how they feel in your hands. Are they heavy or light, sharp or smooth? What is the color, the texture, the consistency etc? It is a fantastic exercise to instantly soothe yourself when emotionally overwhelmed, and you can practice it virtually anywhere.

69
Emotional regulation

Emotional regulation is the process by which we can influence what emotions we have when we have them, and how we experience or express our feelings to others. On a day-to-day basis, we face hundreds of stimuli, and it's unavoidable that some of them are negative. That is when emotional regulation comes into the picture. It acts as a modifier, and it helps us filter these stimuli and respond to them in a way that doesn't evoke stress or fear. Several studies suggest that people with poor emotional regulation strategies are more likely to fall prey to their circumstances and their feelings by not being able to control how they act or react in certain situations. In essence, emotional regulation allows us to determine the outcomes of certain triggering instances by helping us balance and judge what is appropriate for the situation and what isn't.

THE ANXIOUS ATTACHMENT HANDBOOK

Emotional regulation is about pausing between the feeling and the reaction, and the more effective we become at creating a distance, the better we'll be able to understand and communicate our feelings.

To master emotional regulation, we first have to get curious about our feelings and the reactions we respond with in triggering situations. Notice yourself getting worked up, getting disappointed, and feeling let down. Pay attention to your fears and identify the feelings behind them. Observe your thoughts as they come up without attaching any shame, blame, or meaning to them. Instead, reflect to find out the emotion it brings up in you. Don't react to these emotions instantly; label them instead.

70
Is it you or your inner child reacting?

We all have an inner child, a younger version of us who holds our earliest experiences, thoughts, and beliefs about ourselves and the world around us. This inner child represents our developmental stages through life, including how we are in a relationship with others. Depending on how we were cared for, our inner child may have certain degrees of unmet needs, dysfunctional ways of relational bonding, or a lack of trust in oneself and others. When we don't do the healing work to understand better and meet these needs, our inner child can unconsciously sabotage our lives and relationships. So to fully understand why we react the way we do, we need to look at these emotions as being connected to unhealed wounds from our childhood. In order to get there, try to identify where the issue comes from or when it happened in the past. For many of us, it may be challenging to identify these past traumas, especially if we grew up with great parents. An excellent exercise here is to shift our thinking from black and white, good or bad, to a more nuanced way of looking at things. There could be plenty of ways our caregiver's response negatively impacted us in childhood, and we're unaware of them.

These may look like this:

- ➢ Being scolded for weeping or being angry may teach the child that negative emotions aren't acceptable.
- ➢ Being called immature for showing excessive amounts of energy or laughter can teach a child to withhold emotions.
- ➢ Labeling a child's persistence as stubbornness instead of courage may lead to the child resorting to manipulative strategies to achieve their goal.
- ➢ Teaching a child to focus more on the gain rather than the process itself, the play, the journey, and the fun behind being creative, may encourage a competitive mindset that values achievement over effort.
- ➢ Not appreciating a child's unique ways and trying to get them to conform to standard ways or practices may teach them to withhold their authentic self or to learn that differences aren't to be appreciated but frowned upon.
- ➢ Not separating the child's behavior from the child's personality, scolding them using phrases like "You are bad" instead of "What you did was bad" might result in the child internalizing this as a reflection on themselves rather than connecting it to the behavior.

Connecting the dots between your past and present will give you vital clues to your focus areas.

71
Challenge your thoughts

Once you identify the anxious feelings and core wounds, challenge them. Ask yourself if they are your reality, reflect your worth, or are internalized feelings or thoughts from childhood.

This can look like asking yourself the following questions:

- ➢ Is this about my relationship, or is it connected to a deep-rooted insecurity?

➤ Do I really feel unlovable, or did I learn to put myself last as a child?

➤ Does my partner's behavior reflect on me, or is it simply their way of dealing with conflict?

Challenging your thoughts and automatic reactions will open up your perspective, help you see a different version of the same story, and make you more accepting of yourself and others.

72
Reacting vs responding

As anxious attachers, we tend to react harshly and impulsively to situations that make us uncomfortable. A reaction is unconscious and is often an instant consequence of a trigger. It is created based on our internalized beliefs and biases. When we say or do something without thinking it through, that's our unconscious mind running the show.

A reaction is based on the moment and doesn't consider the long-term consequences of what we do or say. A reaction is survival-oriented and, on some level, a defense mechanism. When we react, it's often out of fear. It shows a lack of self-reflection and is motivated by wanting a need met, getting more attention, or closeness. Reacting looks like sudden outbursts of anger: raising our voices, slamming doors, deflecting instead of taking responsibility.

A response usually comes more slowly and is based on information from the conscious and unconscious mind. A response takes into consideration the well-being of not only you but those around you. Responding means reflection and consideration. It considers the long-term consequences of our immediate actions and is influenced by our prefrontal cortex, the logical thinking part of the brain. Responding shows awareness and consideration. It is driven by a need to repair, get closer and deepen the relationship. There is an intentional choice behind responding—the choice of being authentic and open about our emotions, flaws, and triggers.

73
Rewire your trigger reactions

Think of your triggers and trauma reactions and determine which has the most profound impact on your current relationship. Try to be objective when you do this exercise. Shaming or blaming yourself is not going to help the process. The practice is simple. Take one of your anxiously attached patterns, and think about how to turn it around to benefit your relationship. Imagine what you will do differently, what it feels like, and how the change supports your life or partnership. Use any method you like; think it through, talk to your friend or partner about it or simply write it down. I recommend journaling, as it has several proven benefits for anxiety. Journaling will help you process your emotions in a safe, contained space while deepening your understanding of yourself and catching up with your feelings.

Here is an example of the exercise:

The triggering situation: "My partner checks out other people."

My old pattern: "This triggers a deep-rooted anxiety and the core wound of feeling worthless, and I respond by shutting down and giving them the silent treatment."

I will change my reaction by: "Finding ways to boost my self-esteem. I will also take a deep breath when this happens again and let my partner know – in a calm and collected manner – how this behavior makes me feel."

The thought I rewrite in my head: "I'm learning to value my worth by building my self-esteem. I know that my partner loves me and that looking at other people does not impact my worth or my partner's love for me."

The change impacts my life and relationship: "I feel more confident now that I have become more secure in my values. Bringing up the problem to my partner made me realize that my needs and boundaries will not push him away, which feels reassuring."

Practice rewiring your reactions

Focus on exchanging the response to the trigger by associating it with the unbiased truth or a positive thought pattern. Swapping your intrusive thoughts or perceived feelings of a threat to the reality of the situation will help you calm down and leave a positive impact in the long run. The more you practice this corrective emotional experience, the easier it will be to tap into it every time you get triggered.

Intrusive thought	Considered reflection
My partner wants to spend the weekend alone, making me anxious and fearful, as I believe he no longer loves me.	Taking time out of a relationship can be healthy for both of us, and my partner's need for alone time doesn't reflect on me. I will use this time to catch up with my friends and reconnect with myself.
I get anxious whenever I catch my partner checking their phone and smiling. My first reaction is that they are having an affair.	Having close friendships or a great social life outside the relationship is healthy. I believe my partner loves me, is faithful to me, and I don't have any reason to doubt him or our relationship.
I need my partner to reassure me of his feelings and validate my emotions frequently; otherwise, I get overwhelmed and panicked.	My partner is not there to validate all my feelings or to give me constant reassurance. I will learn to validate my emotions and create safety in my life. My partner cares for me even if he doesn't show it daily.

Use common sense and sound judgment when doing this exercise. While I know that separating one's fearful thoughts from reality and noticing what's true and what's created by our anxious brain can be difficult, but by practicing to calm your nervous system, you will achieve great results in the long term. Soothe yourself, reflect, share the problem with your partner, ask for clarification, return to the issue, and reevaluate it from a more relaxed perspective.

74
Being aware of and soothing the different trigger reactions

Successful self-soothing takes practice and self-awareness. You must test and try different methods to learn what works best for you. Here is a list of self-soothing techniques for each sensation:

Feeling numb in your body	Get up and move around, shake down the hands, then the arms, or swing your body from side to side.
Getting a headache or migraine	Stretch your body, arms, and neck, then rub your temples.
Feeling faint or dizzy	Sit down and lay back in a comfortable chair, lie down if it feels good, then take a few deep belly breaths. Inhale, hold, exhale, then inhale again for the count of four. Repeat five times.
Feeling nauseous	Splash some cold water on your face and hold your wrists under cold water.
Racing heart	Take a walk and practice belly breathing. Ensure you take nice long breaths and that the exhale is longer than the inhale. This will regulate your heartbeat.

Breathing difficulties	Go outside and get some fresh air, practice taking long breaths, and work to slow down your breathing by inhaling and exhaling longer with each breath.
Losing focus	Get up and try jumping up and down a few times or shake your arms, legs and body. Try noticing your surroundings through your senses. Note 3 things you can hear, smell, or touch.
Getting restless	Take a calm walk listening to your favorite music, and practice paying attention to your surroundings using only your senses. What colors can you see? How does it feel when your feet touch the ground? What can you smell?
Shaking legs	Get up and walk, move your body, or do a few stretching exercises.
A knot in the stomach	Lay down on your back with your legs pulled up to 90 degrees, then turn your legs from one side to the other. Repeat this for as long as needed.
Stiff muscles	Move around, rotate your body, and swing from side to side. Try doing a few yoga stretches.
Spacing out and dissociating	Cold water exposure helps. Splash cold water on your face or stick your hands into icy water. Hold it there for a few seconds, then repeat it. Use the anchoring technique to ground yourself.

Feeling worked up or angry	Try a breathing technique called the physiological sigh, which involves two inhales, and a long exhale. Take a really deep breath through your nose, then when your lungs are full, try to squeeze in another short breath. Then do a long exhale to the point where your lungs are empty and your stomach flat. Repeat 2-3 times.

75
Practice self-soothing in anticipation of being triggered

I talked about visualizing exercises in an earlier chapter, and this is where it comes into play. Imagine a triggering situation and try to feel all the associated feelings: fear, anger, jealousy, etc. Now think of how you could respond to this situation from a calm and collected space. Imagine what you would do, what you would say, how you would react. Build a framework that suits you. This exercise will help you practice your reactions in anticipation of being triggered. It will solidify the self-soothing process, ensuring you reflect and respond instead of reacting in triggering situations.

A complete self-soothing cycle looks like this:

➤ I'm triggered by my partner's reaction and feel overwhelmed.

➤ I pause before I habitually react.

➤ I take myself out of the triggering situation. I clear my head and return to my body by walking, shaking my arms, splashing cold water on my face, etc.

➤ Then I ask myself where the triggering feeling comes from. Is it based on reality? Is it one of my core wounds?

➣ I acknowledge the feeling and fear behind the trigger and try to rewrite the thought I associate with it: "My partner's reaction doesn't reflect on me. She probably just had a bad day."

➣ I return to my partner when I'm calm and express my feelings.

➣ I ask her to clarify the problem, reassure me if needed, and work to resolve the issue if there is any. (Often, the trigger that comes up has nothing to do with our partner; instead, it's an unhealed core wound.)

➣ I accept the outcome and work to repair our connection or realize what parts of me need healing and make sure to do the work.

Rehearse the situation in your head as often as needed and practice staying calm. Rehearsing your reaction to the triggering event will help you build a solid self-soothing strategy that you can resort to when needed.

76
The process of reparenting

Reparenting describes when an adult works to meet their emotional or physical needs that were unmet in childhood. First developed in the 1970s, reparenting was called transactional analysis. It suggests that we have three ego states that we operate in; parent, adult, and child.

The parent ego state refers to our learned behavior, the thoughts and feelings that are copied, from our parents, caregivers, or other significant adults, like teachers, coaches, or even movie heroes.

The adult ego state works in the present moment and helps us process our feelings and rationally make sense of our thoughts without any interference from our unconscious beliefs. In this ego state, we think and respond appropriately to the situation at hand, displaying logical and consistent behavior. In essence, this is the real us, without interference from the Parent or the Child ego states.

The child ego state is the reenactment of how we behaved, thought, and felt as children. It is not a reference to when we act childish. These behaviors and reactions stem from memories that we cannot remember on a conscious level. These adaptive behaviors can serve as a survival instinct hindering our growth or healing.

When we talk about reparenting, it involves self-reparenting, which suggests that people can overcome reliance on their parent ego state. A person enters their parent ego state and unconsciously adopts mindsets, opinions, or behaviors that mirror their parent's thoughts or behavior. Essentially, a parent ego state is when people act, think, or feel as their parent once did.

This can look like using a lot of negative or critical self-talk, saying things like, "I shouldn't have behaved like that." or "I can't believe I'm this needy.". You might be entering your parent ego state when in distress. But instead of engaging in negative self-talk, you could choose to say, "It's ok that I messed up," or "I'm a good person despite being needy." In other words, you are shifting into your adult ego state, making sense of what happened in a non-judgemental, rational and compassionate way.

You can reparent yourself through a few simple methods, which I will discuss below. **Self-parenting requires intentional work and energy but is a really effective method in rewriting how you view yourself and others.**

77
The essence of self-reparenting

By reparenting yourself, you can tune into all the love, respect, and care you craved but perhaps never received as a child. This process will allow you to feel stable, happy, and balanced. You will become less sensitive to triggers and less likely to seek external validation.

As a first step, **take time to listen to how you speak to yourself.** Do you talk negatively, calling yourself names, belittling, or shaming yourself? Do you repeat the exact phrases in your head? With anxious attachment, our core beliefs are centered around not being good enough, so you might often tell yourself things like

> ➤ "I know I'm not good enough for my partner."
> ➤ "I think my partner deserves someone better than me."
> ➤ "I don't deserve love."
> ➤ "I can't get anything right."

Rewrite your negative self-talk:

Once you find your negative self-talk, replace it with a positive one. Rewiring negative self-talk can happen in many ways, but the quickest and most effective is teaching your brain that the opposite is true. You probably think that positive affirmations will help you. While they are a great way to improve your mood and refocus your attention, they will likely only aid you if they reach your subconscious programming.

So you need to train yourself to find instances when the opposite of the negative thought or your core belief happens, no matter how big or small. Then work to bring your attention to it, internalize it, and feel it. For example, you keep telling yourself that you are unworthy, so you look to find instances when the opposite is proven. Someone gives up their seat for you on a train. Your partner goes shopping and picks up your favorite chocolate without you having to ask. You get a compliment from a stranger. These small instances will help retrain your brain to look for positive cues, proving that the opposite of your core belief is true, and rewrite your limiting, negative thoughts.

So whenever you encounter the opposite of the negative core belief, bring your attention to it and internalize it. Remind yourself how true it is, feel it, and believe it. Connect it to a feeling and let your body remember it. This process is a fantastic way to reprogram yourself to look for cues and teach your body and nervous system that the core belief is false.

Get in touch with your real needs and meet them:

This is a powerful next step in the reparenting process. **Learn to ask yourself your real needs daily and work to meet them.** It might be overwhelming or confusing initially because you are likely wired to neglect your needs to maintain a connection with your attachment figure. But don't get discouraged. Just keep going until it becomes natural.

Say you are having a bad day because your partner must work overtime and cancel the dinner plans. While feeling disappointed is normal, you shouldn't overthink or catastrophize the situation. **Instead, ask yourself what you need to feel safe and reassured without involving your partner.** What could you give yourself to feel better?

Celebrate the small wins:

By focusing on your partner or dates, you likely neglect to notice your success in life. If you were not recognized or celebrated for the unique individual you are, you will quickly disregard the presence of any good that you contribute to your own success.

So keep noticing the small wins. **Establish a routine where you accomplish something small every day. No matter what it is, no matter if it doesn't make sense to anyone else.** Make your bed first thing in the morning, journal every day for 5 minutes, or meditate daily. Recognize once your daily task is done, and give yourself some praise. This will work as a positive reinforcement making it easier to achieve anything the next time.

And most importantly, do not overwhelm yourself. It takes time and daily investment to establish safety in your body, so go slow and recognize the change on your way. Instead of focusing on the big win, notice and celebrate the person you are becoming.

Working on anxious attachment in a relationship

78
What is a securely attached relationship?

When aiming for secure attachment, we must first understand what it is and how it influences our relationships. Securely attached relationships build on understanding and meeting one another's needs, working towards supporting the partner while allowing them to be their authentic self. In secure relationships, the partners rely on and support each other without becoming codependent. They develop problem-solving strategies, de-escalating and reconnecting after a fight, and work towards long-term relationship satisfaction. As securely attached people grow up modeling a positive caregiver relationship, they can replicate a healthy connection with others in all types of relationships. Securely attached people are more social, warm, and easy to connect to. They are in touch with and can express their feelings. They can build deep, meaningful, and long-lasting relationships with others.

Securely attached people are:

- ➤ **Able to demonstrate healthy emotional regulation in a relationship;** they are more likely to remain calm when triggered and respond rather than react
- ➤ **Able to plan** and think in long-term goals with their partner
- ➤ **Great at bonding, opening up to, & trusting others**, as well as letting others in, actively listening to them, and offering support

➤ **Good at communicating their needs effectively**, respecting the needs of their partner, and less likely to trespass on their boundaries

➤ **Comfortable with closeness & mutual dependency**, aren't afraid to ask for or provide help to their partner without pushing in on them or becoming overbearing

➤ **Actively seeking emotional support** from their partner and offering emotional support in return

➤ **Comfortable being alone** or giving their partner time alone when needed

➤ **Able to reflect on how they act in a relationship**, what mistakes they make, and are willing to offer an apology or resolution to problems when needed

79
How to cultivate secure best practices?

Even if you didn't have an upbringing that helped you develop a secure attachment style, it is totally possible to cultivate an earned secure attachment as an adult. It starts with emotional awareness and cultivating the ability to feel safe even when alone.

Here are some key steps:

Learn to identify and express your emotions to yourself and others calmly—no blaming, shaming, pointing the finger, projecting, or stonewalling. Identifying and connecting our feelings with our core needs will be crucial in the learning process. If you recognize the emotion and the need behind it, you create a chance to solve a problem, state a need, or create a boundary. You can then effectively communicate it to your partner and work together to meet each other's needs.

Aim for integrity and look for partners who exhibit it. Securely attached people exhibit behaviors that align with who they say they are and what they say they will do.

Talk about real stuff, and share your relationship concerns with your partner. Be upfront and be brave. Being securely attached doesn't mean you are entirely free of worries, but securely attached folks can easily share their concerns with their partner. This looks like pointing out potential or future problems, sharing your triggers and anxiously attached behavior, and showing up as your most authentic self in the partnership.

Work to discover your patterns, triggers and recognize when your anxious attachment runs the show, and share this with your partner. Let them know what happens when you feel threatened, when you get triggered, and how you act when your attachment system gets activated. Sharing your attachment issues and opening up vulnerably will help your partner understand your anxious attachment activation and give them a cue to co-regulate with you and solve the problem together.

Purge toxic relationships and behavior from your life. Work to reduce the times you are subjected to anything that triggers or sends your nervous system into fight or flight mode. The easiest way to achieve this is to date securely attached people, however, this isn't always possible. So work to reduce the times you get triggered by recognizing what triggers you and laying clear and firm boundaries around this behavior, whether with your partner or yourself. Pay attention to your reactions in triggering situations and learn to recognize them when they happen so that you can leave and self-regulate. Work to limit your time around people or situations that trigger you.

Learn the fine line between leaning on someone for support or validation and being codependent on them. There is a massive difference between healthy co-regulation and codependency. Healthy co-regulation considers the partner's mood and availability and involves consent. Codependency is self-centered. It only focuses on the self, leading with neediness and demands. We have to recognize that our partner isn't there to reassure and validate us, so we need to learn to shoulder some of the responsibility by creating a healthy support system of family and friends and by learning healthy self-regulation and self-validation.

Get curious about your partner. Ask them questions, get to know who they are, and how they make decisions. Learn about their childhood, their past traumas, previous relationships, how they like to relax, and how they solve problems. Don't assume what your partner feels or thinks if there is a problem, miscommunication, or misunderstanding. Ask them to clarify. Talk about needs and boundaries, and work to understand your partner's perspective and thinking. We all come from very different family backgrounds, have different upbringings, and see the world entirely differently. We need to share our versions with each other to avoid conflicts.

Work to understand how you contribute to your relationship dynamics. This applies to both partners. Understanding how and why our behavior impacts our relationship will help us change it and establish mutual ground regarding conflict resolution. Focus on the most common recurring patterns and work to solve or eliminate them first. What is the source of most of your problems? What do you have constant arguments around? Is it spending time together or apart, involving friends in the partnership, communicating (or not) wants and needs, setting boundaries around our resources, or perhaps the availability of our partner? Knowing our part of the equation helps set things right and work through conflict easier, not to mention it can help prevent repeat problems.

80
Core needs and how they show up in our relationships

Core needs in our lives form the basis of every choice, providing us with contentment and satisfaction. If these needs go unmet, the quality of our life will likely diminish, and we will use compensating behaviors to compensate for them in other areas of our lives. There are six core needs, of which the first four are personal. The need for certainty and variety are paradoxes, so if you experience an excess of one, you might find the other one lacking. The same applies to significance and love and connection. For example, if you have an abundance of significance in your life – you're a high achiever, reaching all your career goals – you might find that your personal life or romantic life is lagging. The final two needs, growth and significance are spiritual needs. They provide an essential foundation for fulfillment and happiness.

Need for certainty

This includes stability, consistency, security, control, safety, and predictability. With the need for certainty, we require a sense of stability in our lives. We need to know and understand that there are fixed elements in our lives that we can count on. We need to feel assured that we are safe, that we can avoid hurt, and that our lives and circumstances are predictable.

➢ Wanting to go to the same restaurant
➢ Wanting to keep our job in the long-term
➢ In for long-term partnerships and marriage
➢ Needing a set daily routine
➢ Needing consistent communication and affection
➢ Wanting to feel safe in relationships

Need for variety

The opposite of certainty and it includes the need for variety, challenges, excitement, adventure, change, and novelty. The need for variety calls for change and adventure. It is the need for the unknown and new stimuli, whether it's a new job, a new home, getting to know new people, or going on a trip with our significant other.

- Liking adventure in our partnerships
- Taking the creative approach to our lives
- Celebrating the differences between the partners
- Spending time apart to recharge
- Pursuing individual friendships, hobbies, and goals

Need for significance

This is the need to have meaning in our lives, a sense of importance, feeling needed, wanted, and being worthy of love, etc. Significance is all about knowing that we are seen, that we matter and that we're a priority to our partner. And it's about feeling it too. We experience significance in very different ways. Some of us need a quiet achievement, while others enjoy the spotlight. Either way, this core need centers around feeling unique, special, or needed.

- Needing to feel appreciated in our relationship
- Wanting our partner to voice or show how much they care for us
- Being appreciative of or speaking highly of our partner
- Wanting to feel valued by people around us

Need for love and connection

This is the need for communication, approval, attachment, feeling intimate, and being loved by other human beings. As humans, we need connection. The quality of our connections, friendships, or relationships hugely contributes to our mental and emotional health.

> ➢ Speaking each other's love language
> ➢ Being able to hold conflicting views with kindness
> ➢ Practicing skills of self-awareness
> ➢ Developing skills in emotional intelligence
> ➢ Holding space for vulnerability
> ➢ Healthy co-regulation

Need for growth

More of a spiritual need, it provides a structure for fulfillment and happiness; this is the need for constant spiritual, intellectual, and emotional growth, whether personal or romantic. All adult relationships go through stages of development, and it's crucial to follow along with understanding and compassion. For anxious attachers, accepting the passing of the honeymoon phase can be challenging, as it's our ideal state with heightened emotions and constant contact with our partner. But healthy relationship growth follows each new stage, and we must be open to accepting and appreciating them.

> ➢ Learning a new hobby or exercising together
> ➢ Helping each other grow, heal
> ➢ Teaching one another something
> ➢ Supporting each other through spiritual growth or mastering a new career

Need for contribution

Much like the previous one, this is also a spiritual need, the need to give, care, protect and provide beyond our own needs, the need to give back. By contributing, we hope to improve the lives of others and their physical, mental, or emotional state. If the interaction has made the other person feel better, even in a small way, you contributed to someone else's life.

➤ Giving back on a personal or community level
➤ Supporting our friends and families
➤ Helping our partner, children achieve their life goals
➤ Becoming a parent
➤ Becoming a valuable member of the community
➤ Supporting a good cause
➤ Taking care of our environment
➤ Teaching or coaching others

81
Get clear on your relationship values

Subconsciously, we choose partners who reaffirm our earliest childhood experiences, as our brain recycles old patterns simply because it seeks out the familiar. So to break this pattern, we must be intentional about who we want to date. Start by figuring out what your needs are in a relationship and what a fulfilling relationship means to you. Is it a safe space to grow together, an opportunity to travel and discover new places, or the right support system to help you grow and achieve your goals? A good relationship means something else to all of us, so clarifying what you need in a relationship will simplify the building process.

Before entering the relationship, get clear on your needs, expectations, deal breakers, and boundaries. How would you like to grow, and what would you like to change in yourself? How would you like to be supported by your partner, and how can you support them without overstepping your boundaries? **If you're unaware of your patterns and what you need in a relationship, you are more likely to enter a dynamic that will not serve you in the long run.** Get as straightforward as possible about your non-negotiables, boundaries, triggers, and needs before you approach someone or try dating again. As anxious attachers, it is only too easy to bend our ways for someone and make excuses for their behavior just because we feel an instant chemistry. However, chemistry is not enough. You need your partner's support, understanding, safety, and respect to build a lasting, healthy relationship. So to avoid getting caught up in something that isn't suited for you, you need to know what you are looking for and be able to say no to anything that doesn't serve your needs.

82
Be a little more analytical

This is sound advice if you are beginning a new relationship or just starting to date again. Be a little more analytical about your dates, and instead of trying to get your person to like you, try to figure out if you like them. As anxious attachers, we often get caught up in cycles of people-pleasing, especially at the beginning of a relationship. We ignore our own needs and seek the approval of the other person as a learned behavior to fit in, to be liked and accepted. So instead of focusing on making them like you, try to figure out if they are a good fit for you. Pause, ask yourself how they make you feel, and take your time to assess your feelings.

As it might be difficult for some to figure out how you feel after a first date, here are a few things to focus on. **Ask yourself how you feel being around this person, with the focus being on you.** Were you relaxed, calm, present, and in nice interchange with them, or were you anxious and fidgety? Sometimes we interpret the initial chemistry as a good sign, but sometimes, it is our nervous system pointing to a red flag. Look behind the chemistry, and focus more on connection, compatibility, shared values, openness, self-awareness, and willingness to learn and grow.

83
Resist going all in at the beginning

There is a tendency among anxiously attached people to attach prematurely, to focus all their energies on the new love interest and go all in. Instead, try to go slow when you start dating someone new, and don't neglect other areas of your life. It is easy to get caught up in a new love chapter, but try to hold space for your family, friends, hobbies, workout routine, and everything that makes you happy and fulfilled. This will help you slow down and give yourself time to get to know your person better before committing.

With anxious attachment, we are attracted to a specific type of person, hoping to recreate and resolve an old wound. And therefore, we are quick to believe that we cannot meet suitable people and even faster to attach prematurely. **So it is an excellent practice for anxious people to take it slower than usual and stay open to dating more people. This practice will help remove the pressure of wanting to make something happen with one specific person and keep them from attaching prematurely or putting their date on a pedestal.** Doing this will give you additional time to get to know your person before committing because your attachment system won't get overwhelmed and activated by focusing on one person. Instead, you will stay busy evaluating the options before you.

84
Date with intention.

Stop following your usual trajectory of finding someone and projecting this huge fantasy on them. With anxious attachment, we often become hyper-focused on getting our partner or potential partner to like us, and we seek out people who cannot get our needs met or cannot fully show up to the relationship. That's why dating with intention and getting to know your person is crucial. Instead of falling for people who give you some attention, remind yourself of your needs. What is it you need in a relationship? What are you looking for in a partner? Proceed slowly and carefully, and don't put more trust or reliance on people than the maturity of the relationship would warrant. This way, you will see them for who they are and what they can offer rather than what you project on them.

85
The different stages of a relationship

Every relationship has five main stages: the honeymoon phase, crisis, disillusionment, decision, and authentic love. **Every relationship moves through these five stages, which are more cyclical than linear.** Try to think of these stages as lessons to learn more about yourself and your partner rather than stops to a final destination.

The honeymoon phase is an all-consuming, fresh romance that is the ideal state for the anxiously attached. It is filled with chemistry, giddiness, passion, reciprocity, fun conversations, and fantastic sex. A lot of us mistake these feelings for real love. As the intense emotions drown our rational thinking, we may think we've found the one and are ready to commit fully, giving all we have.

Enjoy this stage fully, but be aware of your heightened emotions. Take time to step back and observe your partner, the relationship, and whether this person is the best match for you. Try paying attention to their red flags as well as yours, and work to stay mindful of your needs and relationship preferences.

In the crisis stage, the intense chemistry wears off, and we start to notice our differences, our partner's flaws. The qualities we used to find endearing begin to annoy us, and different power struggles start to set in. With disappointment, our anxiety and stress levels also escalate, and the frictions start pushing us apart.

Fundamental conflict management skills are crucial at this stage. Remember that power struggles and arguments are standard parts of a relationship; they're not necessarily a sign that love is ending, or the relationship isn't working. Learn to notice and appreciate your differences in opinion. Let your partner be their most authentic self, and strive to be that yourself.

The third stage of a relationship is the **disillusionment stage**, which is the winter season of love. This may feel like the end of for some couples. At this point, the power struggles have become fully and painfully apparent, and the problems the couple has tried to sweep under the rug have resurfaced. It is more common to argue, fight, or distance at this stage, and every couple experiences it slightly differently, depending on their temperament.

There might be a lot of negative energy in the relationship at this stage, so work to clear the air and offer each other space and opportunity to share openly, state needs, distance yourselves if needed, and show each other affection. During this stage, our brain is zeroing in on the defects of the relationship, so work to actively see the best both in your partner and your partnership.

At **the decision stage,** you're at your breaking point. It is common to have emotional breakdowns and spend time apart. Self-protective behaviors and **anxious activating strategies, and protest behaviors are common.** Indifference and remoteness are frequent.

At this stage, learning effective and clear communication is more crucial than ever, as years of built-up resentment or disappointment can fade by voicing them the right way. **It is best to do inner work or try counseling at this stage before you make a final decision and reevaluate your partnership**, as even if you decide to part ways, it'll be more constructive and amicable.

The last stage of our relationship is **authentic love,** the healthiest and most rewarding of all. Couples experience self-discovery and acceptance, both towards themselves and their partner. The work needed at this phase changes as both partners recognize the need to listen and give without feeling threatened or attacking one another. In this stage, couples also begin to play together again. They can laugh, relax, and sincerely enjoy each other, almost like in the honeymoon phase.

Put self-care and growth center stage here, and learn to sustain your love for each other with acceptance and compassion.

86
The beginning of the relationship and its triggers

It is all too easy to be in the beginning phase of a relationship for those of us with anxious attachment, as intense intimacy, frequent conversations, and closeness is the ideal state for us. While it is really easy to give it all we have and overstep our boundaries, we must remind ourselves to take things slow. This period is usually characterized by a constant high where we can easily get carried away by the other person's feelings, reactions, and how they treat us.

Focusing on who we are and our boundaries and core values is crucial in this period. It's also essential to hold space for what makes us feel safe and sound—friends, family, hobbies, wellness, and work. Stepping back and assessing the relationship more neutrally can help us see if it fits our needs. Communicating our fears and boundaries will also help us and the other person make a more informed and rational decision about the expectations we'll face later on. So while we can easily get carried away at the beginning, it's important to hold true to ourselves through self-awareness and honest communication to avoid falling into the familiar pattern of going all in without assessing whether our person is suitable.

87
Mixed signals and how to interpret them

Communication is the foundation of our relationships. Still, in a new romance, deciphering what our partner is trying to say can often be tricky. **In a romantic context, mixed signals are when a partner simultaneously expresses interest and a lack of interest.** This can be highly confusing and triggering for someone with anxious attachment, as this reminds them of the inconsistent parenting behavior they grew up with. This can trigger several core wounds, pushing our attachment system into activation.

Overall, mixed signals do not indicate that you need to change, but rather the person sending the signals has some inner work to do. So here are the most common mixed signals we can receive in the early dating phase:

- Frequent communication without any willingness to make plans. You meet someone and exchange numbers, and messages go back and forth, but there is never any mention of an actual date or meeting in person.
- Inconsistency and unavailability. This happens when you spend time with someone but never hear from them between those meetings. They never initiate calls or arrange to meet up with you, and all the planning falls on you. The only reassurance you get is the rare time you spend with this person.
- Expressing a need for a more profound emotional connection but never actually going deeper. This looks like promising to want a committed, closer relationship but pulling out or failing to show up for the partner when it's time for heavier topics or a more serious commitment, e.g., meeting friends or family. There is usually a fear of being vulnerable behind this and of opening up to 'unknown and scary feelings.'

➢ Only showing up when it's convenient for them. These people may promise to want to go all in, but they're only available when it's convenient for them. For example, they tell you that you can turn to them with your problems, but they avoid hard conversations or limit their interactions with you to lighthearted fun times.

➢ Honeymoon period, followed by a drastic change. This can occur when someone keeps in touch with you regularly, texts you frequently, meets you often, then suddenly dramatically changes their behavior, ghosts you, or starts treating you poorly, hoping you will pull the plug on the connection.

While mixed signals can be incredibly confusing and frustrating on the receiving end, we have to keep in mind that the person sending these signals might be battling their inner conflict (mother/father wound, recent breakup trauma, avoidant attachment style, etc.), and is often unaware of their inconsistent behavior. The best way to deal with this inconsistency is to keep open communication. It will help you understand each other's needs better and avoid conflict. On the other hand, if this behavior negatively impacts your mental or emotional health or overall sense of self-worth, then it's time to assess whether it's worth staying in the situation.

88
The maturing phase of the relationship and its triggers

The maturing of a relationship is a natural and inevitable process that all partnerships go through. While most people react to this phase with empathy and understanding, it can cause severe emotional distress for the anxiously attached. It is a time that most anxiously attached people see as a perceived threat due to the routine setting in and the declining sexual or emotional affection. Some of us might start reading too much into our partner's declining need for intimacy or the fact that the topic of conversation shifts from exciting to routine. In most cases, there is no reason to fear. Try keeping the focus on quality time together and prioritizing each other's needs. Frequent check-ins and arranging regular date nights can help you feel more at ease. Try shifting the focus on keeping the spark alive, learning a new hobby, exercising, hiking, and spending time together regularly. As always, communicating and respecting each other's needs and boundaries should remain center stage.

89
The ending of the relationship and its triggers

Breakups can be incredibly devastating for those of us anxiously attached because we are really invested in our relationship; we give it our all. So when the relationship ends, a part of us dies with it. This is the phase when our activating strategies kick in, and we tend to lose ourselves in the grief and the loss. Activating strategies can range from putting our ex-partner on a pedestal, fantasizing about them returning, to thinking this was our only chance at love. We may even try to attract their attention by calling, texting, or releasing social media posts just to evoke a reaction. We can also jump straight back into other relationships, as it gives us a sense of safety and completion. As anxiously attached, we tend to draw our value from relationships, as that's where we get most of our needs met. So we often go back to unhealthy relationships simply because the familiarity feels safer – even if it's dysfunctional – than being alone.

90
Anxious attachment and breakup recovery

While you have been dealing with breakups a certain way for a long time, remember there is another way. You can learn to handle the separation with grace and learn the steps you can take to face its challenges. Try to focus on yourself, and while it might be difficult, ground yourself in the realization that you are whole and complete even when alone. Feel all your feelings, don't try to fantasize your way out of the painful emotions, and don't compartmentalize. Take this time to focus on your needs and your personal growth. However harsh it sounds, a breakup is an excellent opportunity to evaluate a phase in our lives and learn from our mistakes. Don't be hard on yourself, and don't shame or blame yourself for your flaws; instead, look at them objectively. Give yourself some extra love and care, meditate daily, journal about your feelings, and try to enjoy being with yourself. There is no right or wrong after a breakup. So don't punish yourself for the fear, pain, anger, or other emotions that may come up. Instead, take this opportunity as a space to grow in order to build a healthier partnership the next time around and give yourself some true self-care.

91
How to rebuild ourselves after a breakup?

Recognizing that the relationship has reached a no-turning-back point is incredibly painful, and ending it is even more so. So when it happens, it is vital to let the recovery period run its course before we start the healing process. Anxiously attached people have difficulties with being alone, which often results in wanting to go back to the ex or jumping into a rebound relationship. These rebound relationships fail almost always because they often reflect whatever pieces you felt were missing from your last relationship. So put it simply, you attempt to fill a void without giving yourself time to heal, learn and recognize who you are and what you need. In this case, the rebound partner serves as a means of making up for your past relationship's mistakes. By the time you move through the transition of closure, your relationship with the rebound inevitably changes.

So to avoid being hurt and hurting another person, it is best to acknowledge the need for the healing process and let the grieving phase play out. Create a safe place to explore and get grounded if you feel overwhelmed. This might be an actual place, a friend, a daily routine, or going to the gym. Start developing ways that will enable you to become more self-reliant. Start validating your feelings, thoughts, and decisions. Rebuilding your sense of self, confidence, and identity should be your focus in this period. Be sure to surround yourself with people you trust to help you on your journey; friends, family, and a therapist can help provide the stability you need to heal and grow. Are you big on daily routines? Try one! Set up a simple daily practice that gives you comfort and familiarity, and keep to it. This could be a daily walk, a delicious morning coffee, or journaling. Be intentional about your future self. You are going through some inevitable change, so be selective about what you bring and leave behind. And finally, trust the process.

92
Letting go of past hurt and practicing forgiveness

I would like to preface this chapter by saying that forgiveness is optional. You don't have to forgive or forget to move on and find peace or closure after a breakup, but letting go of past hurts will help you immensely in the healing process. And while it might be tempting to hold a grudge against our wrongdoer, and it might even feel like we are holding them accountable, in most cases, it's not worth our emotional health or inner peace.

If you decide to forgive someone, it doesn't let them off the hook or minimize the impact of their actions on your life. However, it might bring you peace and possibly even relief from the negative emotions and thoughts you hold on to. This might help you reach the much-needed release from all the anxious thoughts, ruminating and replaying past situations or conversations in your head over and over. With anxious attachment, it is pretty common to experience an 'external forgiveness.' This type of forgiveness is spoken or expressed outwards only, and it doesn't reflect a sense of relief from negative emotions, such as anger and hurt. So we often hold onto past hurts, even long after the breakup. Releasing these negative emotions through forgiveness might help us speed up the healing process and find a better footing in our next relationship without holding onto grudges or expecting our new partner to make up for the ex's mistakes.

Letting go of past hurts doesn't mean acknowledging you were the victim. It makes you much stronger, more resilient, and one step closer to securely attaching in your next relationship. Releasing your emotional baggage will help you concentrate on the way forward and give you space to deal with your healing rather than constantly thinking about what if and why. This will prevent accumulating more emotional baggage that we carry into the next relationship and refocus the attention on us.

How to create your ideal relationship with anxious attachment?

93
Creating your ideal relationship

Creating your ideal relationship starts by figuring out what it is and working out a relationship blueprint that will serve as a guideline. A relationship blueprint is a simple template that helps both partners feel more loved, appreciated, and respected. It can include what you want to share with each other, what you need from one another on a physical or emotional level, what boundaries you would like to set in the relationship, and how you would like to communicate with each other. It can also include conflict resolution, your preference for receiving love, plans for the future, and shared values.

It might sound very structured, but a relationship blueprint is there to help us navigate the ups and downs. It helps with disappointments, misunderstandings, and differences in opinion. **It sets some ground rules that a couple can follow should they encounter a triggering situation or a conflict, which, let's face it, is inevitable.** And when that happens, it is easier than you think to fall back into the familiar patterns of miscommunication, shutting down, or acting out. That's when a blueprint comes in handy, for it helps each partner navigate conflict and resolve the problem.

To create a healthy relationship, you must first figure out what it is. It's important to consider what patterns we picked up in childhood, what triggers us, and what went wrong in our past relationships, and then we should think about how we would like to continue. If you need, circle back to chapter 52 and recheck your recurring relationship patterns. We all have an ideal relationship in mind. Most of us, anxious attachers, grew up with an unhealthy idea of what a healthy relationship dynamic is, and we keep subconsciously reinforcing this in our private lives. As children, we model our parent's relationship simply because that's the first of its kind we ever know. If you are anxiously attached, chances are your parent, or primary caregiver was too, so picking up the same relational dynamics, communication strategies, or protest behaviors isn't surprising. So why don't you start by clarifying your patterns, understanding what holds you back from living your best life with your partner, and thinking about how you would like to continue? Here are a few questions to help you start:

If you were to design your ideal relationship, what would it look like?

- ➢ What values do you want to build it on?
- ➢ What are the most critical topics to discuss?
- ➢ How do you want to give and receive love in your relationship?
- ➢ What boundaries would you set with yourself and your partner?
- ➢ What are your needs and must haves?
- ➢ What would serve as the foundation of the relationship?
- ➢ What would you like to heal in yourself for a better connection?
- ➢ What negative patterns will you leave behind?

In earlier chapters, we discussed recurring patterns that keep coming up in each past relationship standing between us and a fulfilling partnership. We all have something holding us back from reaching our relationship goals. For some, it's our core wounds and internalized shame; for others, it's our insecurities and fear of being let down again. **What is it for you? What prevents you from having your ideal relationship?**

94
What would you change in yourself for a better relationship?

A healthy and secure relationship starts with changing our thought patterns and reactions by controlling our anxious behavior through self-soothing. It's not only easier to change ourselves, but by setting the right example, we could encourage our partner to do the same. So why don't you start by thoroughly evaluating your anxiously attached patterns and figuring out what needs to be changed and what is a priority? There are several fears connected to our core wounds, so list them all out and see which one is a priority for you: fear of being unlovable, being alone, being rejected, being powerless, worthless, or incomplete. Once you identify your fears, list out all the behaviors connected to them.

Here is an example of how:

I fear	To avoid this
Being abandoned,	I attach to people prematurely I am overly clingy with my partners, I give beyond my comfort zone
Being worthless,	I fix my partner's problems I work hard to earn love I never say 'no' I choose partners who I need to prove my worth to
Being rejected,	I am always agreeable I don't speak my needs I let my partner overstep my boundaries I don't speak my needs

95
Involve your partner in the healing process

Co-healing is a beautiful practice that can help bring you closer to your partner and create a deeper connection. When you improve the health of your relationship, you also improve your mental and physical health. Enhancing your relationship looks like understanding each other's needs, having open communication about what each of you can or cannot tolerate, making sure your actions match your words, not expecting your partner to meet all of your needs, and allowing them to go through difficult times without trying to save them or solve their problems. When done right, you will establish trust and appreciation for each other, providing the stability and security from which you can grow.

96
Learn about your partner's past and relationship habits

It takes two to make or break a partnership, and learning about your partner's relationship patterns helps shed light on the dynamics of your partnership. In any relationship, you are only one-half of the solution. You can better understand your relationship if you know your partner's habits, patterns, traumas, needs, and boundaries better. It can help identify the strong points in the relationship and point out the areas that need more attention. So try to look at your partner without judgment and determine how they contribute to your partnership. Is your partner great at problem-solving? Are they open to communication and sharing their feelings? Are they empathizing with your issues? Can they relate to your attachment style? Are they expressive of their needs and boundaries? Are they self-aware?

97
What to share with your partner?

A relationship blueprint is nothing but a set of guidelines we aim to follow throughout our partnership to ensure we communicate clearly and lovingly; we can handle conflict and repair after a fight, and we respect and actively work towards meeting each other's needs. A good blueprint includes topics that directly or indirectly impact your relationship, like how you interact with your partner, resolve conflict, meet each other's needs, and your love preferences. **For this, partners should discuss childhood and relationship history, love preferences, past relationship setbacks and problems, sexual desires, and plans for the future.**

Early family dynamics, childhood traumas, and upbringing significantly impact our lives and, consequently, our adult relationships. The more you know about each other, the better you can navigate triggers, work around each other's needs and understand why you do what you do. Depending on the type of care available to us, we each developed different strategies to cope and stay safe in our families. These can be isolating when we feel overwhelmed, dismissing deep emotions, disconnecting from others just to feel the instant need to reconnect again, becoming clingy and needy to self-soothe, or using subtle ways of manipulation to keep our partners close. Awareness of these patterns and how and why they developed can help you better understand your partner and navigate the hardships in the relationship.

Relationship history is equally important to share, especially major relationship events. What worked and what didn't, what challenges you each faced, and how you would like to work on this in your current partnership. Our past relationships form how we enter the next ones, how we relate to our new partners, how we behave, and what we allow into our lives. In order to move forward and start things on a healthy note, share your past relationship hiccups, where things went wrong, and whether there was a setback. Were there continuous disagreements around a particular topic or a recurring problem?

Love preferences. Everyone has a choice for how they want to give and receive love; the more you share this with your partner, the more fulfilling your relationship will become. **Talk about your preferences**

in love. But instead of categorizing them into love languages, be specific. Name things, point them out, or tell your partner if they did something you appreciate. There is immense pressure on us to show up with grand romantic gestures, while we neglect to show praise, appreciation, and gratitude for our partner daily. So sharing your love language doesn't have to be exclusive to sexual or physical preferences. Do you love your partner bringing your favorite coffee to bed every morning? Share it with them and show appreciation when they show up for you.

Past relationship difficulties. When it comes to **relational challenges**, be as open as possible. Talk about your triggers, your past relational patterns, and mess-ups. What happens when you are triggered? How do you handle conflict, and how do you resolve it? Tell each other how you react in the face of disappointments, how you approach problems, how well and how often you can or want to share your emotions. Practice active listening and work towards an easy resolution to these problems.

This sounds very basic, but trust me, most couples never let each other in on their emotional needs; however, this is vital in getting to know your partner. It also helps you learn more about one another and understand why you act and react as you do. Here are some examples:

Early family dynamics and childhood traumas	"My father left us when I was little, and I am fearful that people will abandon me. This makes me act clingy and needy every time you pull away, as I fear you will leave too." "My mom kept scolding me for being needy, so I learned to be independent and have difficulty letting others help me or asking for help."

Relationship history	"I was cheated on in my last relationship, and it made it difficult for me to trust others, even when I know I can." "In my last relationship, we never really shared our deepest feelings and avoided discussing emotional topics. So it takes time for me to open up and share things with you."
How we want to give and receive love,	"I would love to spend more quality time with you; going to the theatre or exploring the country over the weekends would be nice options." "I don't feel comfortable being touched like that. It makes me feel uncomfortable."
Relational challenges	"I have a hard time opening up to my partners in a relationship. I would like to take it slow." "I like to deal with problems and not let them fester. My approach is to talk about everything and meet each other halfway."

98
What to include in your relationship blueprint?

What your needs are in a relationship. Discuss how you like to receive love, what your attachment style is, what your love language is, how you imagine your life together, what your needs are on a daily, weekly, monthly basis, how you would like to include your partner in your life, how do you imagine living together.

> ➢ "I love it when we are in touch throughout the day, it makes me feel reassured."
> ➢ "I am not ready to move in together yet, but I love spending the evenings with you and I would love to split our time between my place and yours."

What your relationship challenges are. Talk about your triggers, your past relational patterns, and mess ups, your core wounds, what happens when you are triggered, how you handle conflict, how you resolve conflict, how you handle disappointment, how you approach problems, how well and how often you can share your emotions.

> ➢ "When we get into an overheated fight, I need us to take a break and cool off. Then get back to the discussion when we are both calm."
> ➢ "I can't handle problem-solving and shut down in the face of conflict. If you could try and give me reassurance and compassion, I'm sure I could work out things with you better."

How you want to handle conflict. Discuss what happens when one of you gets triggered, overreacts, or flips out. Fights and disagreements are inevitable, no matter how compatible we are with our partners. So lay down some ground rules for handling conflict and difficult conversations, and set the tone for potential arguments.

> ➢ "I would like you to keep your voice down when we get into an argument, because raised voices scare me."
> ➢ "When we fight, I get so overwhelmed that I say things I don't

mean, so I will just step away, cool off, and continue when I'm regulated."

How you support each other through your attachment problems. Awareness of each other's attachment needs and helping each other is a great way to build connection and security in your partnership. Share as much about your attachment style as you feel comfortable, and don't be afraid to be vulnerable with your partner. Remember, this is a partnership, and for it to work, you'll have to be open about what is holding you back so you can do your best to meet each other's needs. Encourage them to discover their attachment style or past patterns that can contribute to the relationship dynamic.

> ➤ My anxious attachment makes me very insecure about time spent apart, and I would appreciate it if we kept checking in with each other even when we're not together.

How you both like to receive love. Knowing each other's love language is not the goal here. Try to be more specific. Tell your partner what makes you happy and comforted, what you love, and what you can't tolerate. Be clear and intentional. If you like the way they make your morning coffee let them know. Ask for it if you want to be touched or held more frequently. Remember, asking for your needs to be met will help your partner take the guesswork out of the equation. Couples who understand each other's love language and show love and affection in their partner's preferred way report a higher overall relationship satisfaction.

What your long-term goals are. Figuring out if your long-term goals match can be very encouraging. On the other hand, if your plans for the future don't align, knowing it as soon as possible saves both of you time and heartache. I realize it can be intimidating to have an open conversation about this, but you deserve to have your relationship needs met, so lead with courage and an open mind. And remember, if someone tells you they are not looking for anything serious, believe them. You don't have to try and change, save, or fix anyone, prove your worth, or earn love.

Negative patterns. It is inevitable for both partners to bring some negative patterns into the relationship dynamic, and the sooner you share this, the sooner you will understand each other's actions and reactions. This will help prevent conflict and better understand each other's responses.

Including friends in your lives. Keep an open discussion around having mutual friends. Discuss whether you have a separate group of friends and how you want to include them in your relationship. Do you have friendships with the gender you're attracted to? Is that allowed? What are your needs around spending time with friends? Another topic worth discussing here is being friends with an ex if that is allowed, and if so, what boundaries would you like to create around this?

Time spent together and apart. This is an important topic to cover, especially as structure and a healthy timeline can give the anxiously attached peace of mind. Discussing how much time you spend together and apart will help manage your expectations and keep things relatively straightforward. Perhaps one of you needs more time alone. How will you handle this? When will you move in together? If you live together, how do you ensure that you both have a healthy 'me' time?

99
Learn about each other's attachment style

It's important to mention here that diagnosing or labeling your partner as an insecure attachment is not the goal here. While it's absolutely okay to wonder about our partner's attachment style or analyze them, we should not make assumptions based on this, draw consequences about their personality, or try to predict their future reactions or the outcome of our relationship. Instead, ask questions, get curious about their childhood, ask them to take a test, or look into the topic.

A relationship with an anxiously attached partner

The connection between two anxious partners can be pretty fulfilling, as they share similar values and have similar relationship needs. **They both value connection, quality time, and sharing their emotions openly. They can resolve problems as they arise and seek help as needed.** This compatibility keeps their attachment style under control for some time. But these two people can quickly become codependent on one another, losing their sense of self in the relationship, with personal boundaries becoming unclear, resulting in enmeshment. This partnership also has the potential to become controlling, as both partners heavily rely on each other to meet one another's needs. Anxiously attached people aren't naturally drawn to each other. They usually prefer someone on the opposite end of the spectrum. However, there are steps that you can take to make this dynamic better. If your partner is anxiously attached, make sure you keep healthy boundaries with each other, learn to be more self-reliant, and keep a healthy social life outside the relationship to avoid becoming too dependent on each other. Challenge your insecurities and have frequent conversations about them with your partner. They will appreciate openness, honesty, vulnerability, and solving problems together.

Communicating with an anxious partner

Anxiously attached people can be great listeners; they can initiate conversations and be present; however, when triggered, they quickly internalize anything you say. So when speaking to your anxious partner, be mindful of what you say and how you say it. The anxious partner is often full of insecurities and jumps to conclusions quickly, so reassuring language and tone will help you when discussing anything with them. Trust is key. Show them they can trust you by giving them context and reassurance, and be sure to follow up with your words.

> ➤ "I will be working late tonight and don't know when I'll finish,

but I'll text you as soon as I'm on my way home."
- ➤ "I know you need reassurance from me, but you should know that I care for you even if I don't show it all the time."

Anxious people constantly need to stay connected, so try to acknowledge this and make an effort to keep in touch or tell them if you can't. Don't leave things unaddressed, as it triggers their fear of rejection and abandonment. Reassure your partner that your different needs have nothing to do with them, and it's completely normal to want different things in a relationship. It doesn't mean rejection or drifting apart. And finally, if you feel that your partner is becoming overwhelmed, offer to co-regulate with them. They will be delighted to get a hug as reassurance of your love.

A relationship with a disorganized partner

This is a powerful pairing with many similarities and a great potential for a fulfilling love life. A fearful avoidant shares both anxious and avoidant traits, so they share many similarities with their anxious partner. They both value deep intimacy, closeness, openness, and an emotional connection. Generally speaking, they're very well-attuned. Their problems begin when the relationship progresses, as there is a new level of commitment and expectations, while the initial intimacy and ease fade. The fearful-avoidant starts zeroing in on their activating and deactivating strategies, and this inconsistent behavior triggers the anxious partner. There is also a lack of boundaries here, and the built-up codependency in the relationship triggers the fearful partner to back out. This, in return, triggers the anxious partner to get closer, resulting in a spiral of unhealthy push and pull. If you find yourself in this dynamic, remember there is a lot of potential for a fulfilling relationship. Learn to set and respect healthy and flexible boundaries

Communicating with a disorganized partner

Fearful avoidant partners have a deeply internalized fear of rejection paired with the need to get close to their significant other. They are guarded and very protective of themselves, which can cause them to shut down or get defensive if the conversation turns to them, or if they feel blamed or shamed by their partner. Remember, they share both anxious and avoidant characteristics, and they may switch between wanting openness and honesty but quickly shut down in the face of emotional pressure. Their deep-rooted fear of betrayal can make them super skeptical about anything you say, making them dissociate during conversations. **These people are susceptible to language and tone of voice and can easily pick up inconsistencies or changes in your body language.** So when addressing a problem, use 'I' statements and explain the issue from your point of view. Be present, patient and use reassuring words. Try to be their safe person and validate their experience while holding space for your needs. Don't blame or shame them for their needs or reactions. Fearful avoidants may have faced negative consequences of expressing emotions or being their authentic self in childhood, and they can easily get threatened if a similar situation triggers them.

A relationship with an avoidantly attached partner

This couple is on the other end of the spectrum in their behaviors and has an incredible capacity to balance each other out, holding up a mirror for one another. Avoidants bring logic and planning into the partnership, while the anxious add emotional depth and encourage their partner to show up vulnerably. These partners can learn a lot from each other if they manage to get through each other's protective barriers. The avoidant shows the anxious partner how to approach problems calmly and logically, communicate directly, and be more self-reliant. The anxious partner teaches their avoidant how to tap into their emotions, be more empathetic and express their needs and feelings more consistently. Their relational problems arise because they are polar opposites of each other. While the avoidant needs space to self-regulate, the anxious needs closeness and reassurance. While the avoidant often shuts down in the face of conflict, the anxious partner is vulnerable and open to addressing issues and discussing feelings. These differences make the anxious partner think that their avoidant doesn't love them enough, while the avoidant believes they are a disappointment or failed their partner. These two seek out their unmet childhood needs in each other, hoping to heal them through the relationship. While it's entirely possible, they often fall into the so-called 'anxious-avoidant conflict cycle' and end the relationship prematurely. If your partner is avoidantly attached, learn to give them space to regulate their nervous system, give them plenty of reassurance, and strive to build a great support system outside the partnership. This will help ease the pressure on your avoidant, allowing them to consider the relationship a safe space.

Communicating with an avoidant partner

Avoidant people are sensitive to feelings of inadequacy or not being good enough and are to jump to conclusions if you attack them. **So with avoidants, you must pick the right time and way to speak your needs; otherwise, they will internalize what you say and think the problem is them.** Taking agency of your feelings helps your avoidant partner to see both sides of the equation without assuming they are the problem. Use non-threatening language and speak from your perspective. Again, 'I' statements will help you find the right tone. Avoidants like clarity and logic. Their thinking is a little more black and white than that of anxious people, and they often need examples as they may have difficulties understanding your perspective. They work well with direct communication as they struggle to read between the lines. They also prefer to see a solid action plan, which helps them follow through easier. Don't expect them to volunteer to start a conversation, though. They tend to compartmentalize their thoughts and bury their feelings deeply. Giving them enough time to open up and connect with you will help ease some of the communication difficulties. They need to feel safe to open up completely, which takes longer than any attachment style. Avoidants need to learn how to express and accept displays of emotions in a relationship, as they didn't have a great model growing up. You can help them by explaining that your needs and asks are normal in a relationship, showing them that co-regulation is a fantastic way to stay connected, and encouraging them to talk about their feelings because you won't judge or dismiss them. Be patient, kind, reassuring, and compassionate. These folks need time to catch up with your emotional readiness, so don't get discouraged if you see a slow process.

A relationship with a securely attached partner

I'd like to preface that a securely attached partner is no guarantee for a successful relationship. **However, being with someone securely attached gives most anxious people a safe space for healing without being triggered.** Research shows that people with a predominantly secure attachment style respond differently to relationship challenges. They have healthy ways of coping with anxiety and relational problems. They can give and take space without feeling rejected, set and respect clear boundaries and develop interdependence in relationships.

An anxious attacher has a lot to learn from a secure partner. They can provide a safe space to regulate emotions, heal traumas, and unlearn your dysfunctional communication styles. It doesn't mean that secure people can be put through anything or used as a 'tool for healing,' but they are more likely to understand and support you or call you out on your bad behavior with love and kindness. Also worth mentioning that as our attachment styles are not fixed and securely attached people can shift towards insecure attachment traits when facing traumatic events or when triggered.

100
The anxious-avoidant conflict cycle

Conflict and disagreements happen in every relationship, even between securely attached partners. However, navigating the anxious-avoidant dynamic can be particularly challenging because these partners trigger each other's core emotional wounds. Both partners have increased emotional sensitivity to relational threats, but this shows up differently.

The anxious partner's core belief of rejection and abandonment is triggered by the avoidant partner's lack of emotional attunement and deactivating strategies. During the conflict, they may feel alone and unimportant, like they don't matter to their partner, and this pain can be incredibly intense. The anxious partner's internal safety is deeply rooted in their relational safety as they draw a sense of security from their partner's presence and availability. So when conflict arises, their so-called protest behaviors kick in, and they start engaging in often dysfunctional behaviors to re-establish the connection. Their only way to return to a normal state and a regulated nervous system is by re-establishing the connection, which gives them safety.

Anxious protest behaviors include criticism, blaming, becoming even more clingy, subtle ways of manipulation, escalating conflict, demands, empty threats, and acting hostile.

For the avoidant partner, the anxious person's over-dependence, lack of respect for personal boundaries, and seemingly needy behavior combined with demands and criticism feel threatening. They fear losing their autonomy; they feel smothered and often suffocated. Avoidantly traded people crave emotional intimacy but most likely were punished or ignored when showing emotions, so they deem them unsafe. When facing heightened emotions, their strategy is to disengage, disconnect and dismiss their partner and the longing for a deep connection with another person. When they face criticism, they internalize it and start assuming the problem is them, seeking a solution the only way know how, by isolation and disconnection. Their only way to return to a regulated nervous system is to disconnect, isolate, withdraw, and shut down.

Avoidant deactivating strategies are getting defensive, shutting down, isolating, getting critical, stonewalling, projecting, distancing, and even breaking up.

The trigger cycle in the anxious-avoidant dynamic:

- ➤ A triggering event happens
- ➤ The anxious partner fears abandonment and rejection and reacts from an activated place
- ➤ Their reaction is confrontation, blaming, shaming, or criticism
- ➤ The avoidant partner fears to be vulnerable, fears for their autonomy, and being threatened
- ➤ They get dysregulated and become dismissive, they withdraw from the situation and avoid the partner
- ➤ The anxious partner shows protest behaviors
- ➤ The avoidant partner gets triggered even more, and their deactivating strategies kick in
- ➤ Both partners feel hurt, invalidated, and their core attachment wounds get reaffirmed

101
What is a boundary?

A boundary is a healthy guideline we create to protect ourselves, our well-being, and our autonomy. Boundaries can help us retain a sense of identity and personal space, and they're easier to create and maintain than one might think. Setting boundaries means asking our partner to meet our needs and respecting our choices in life and the relationship. Establishing and maintaining boundaries as anxiously attached can be difficult, for we are predisposed to believe that people will not respect them. So we either don't set any or hold onto inflexible ones. It is perfectly healthy and normal to have needs, and it doesn't make us clingy, wrong, or demanding.

First, let's clarify our relationship needs; reassurance, validation, connection, or perhaps all of these. This will help determine whether our partner is truly compatible with us and help verbalize the boundaries more clearly.

102
Types of boundaries

There are different types of boundaries based on our physical, mental, and emotional needs, and keeping tabs on them will lead to a more fulfilled life.

Physical boundaries include everything you might need physically. This could be personal space, comfort, physical touch, rest, nourishment, etc. These boundaries are one of the easiest to overstep, especially when two people live together, and it's challenging to carve out healthy space or alone time.

With anxious attachment, physical boundary violations can feel like not being embraced enough by our partner, having physical distance between us, e.g., a long-distance relationship, or being pushed away. Having a third person come between the partners (a friend or colleague) can also feel frightening, as this gives the feeling of physically taking away from the connection.

Setting physical boundaries can sound like

- ➢ "I don't want you to touch me like that. It makes me feel uncomfortable."
- ➢ "Please, don't go into my room without asking first."
- ➢ "I am not a big hugger. I would prefer to shake hands with your friends."
- ➢ "I feel a distance between us. I would like a hug to reassure me."
- ➢ "I get anxious when we are physically apart. Can we find a

way to connect even when you're traveling?"

It is important to mention the physical boundary violations that anxiously attached people can be guilty of. These include not giving enough space to our partners, pushing in on their private time with friends, frequently checking in with them, or monitoring their whereabouts.

Emotional boundaries are about respecting each other's feelings, commitment, and energies in a partnership. Setting healthy emotional boundaries is about recognizing how much emotional energy you can give or take. Respecting emotional boundaries includes validating others' feelings as well as your own and respecting their ability to take in information without shaming or blaming them.

This can trigger anxious attachment, especially when we are dating someone who is emotionally less available or articulate than we are. This is often upsetting, as we can naturally conclude that our partner doesn't understand and value us or that they invest less in the relationship than we do.

Setting emotional boundaries can sound like

- ➤ "Getting criticized when sharing my feelings makes me really upset. I don't want to share anything with you unless you can respond respectfully and work to understand me."
- ➤ "I am so sorry you are having such a tough time. I don't have the emotional capacity to take that in right now. Do you think we can come back to this some other time?"
- ➤ "I am having a hard time not knowing where we stand in the relationship. Can we discuss this so I know what to expect?"
- ➤ "It makes me feel anxious when you pull away. Do you think that instead of dismissing the problem, we could find a time to talk about it?"

Emotional boundary violations for the anxiously attached can be a partner criticizing their feelings or dismissing the problems or needs they share with them. It can also be a partner not validating their feelings or not responding to their need for emotional closeness.

On the other hand, anxiously attached people can overstep their partner's boundaries by asking questions that are not appropriate for the relationship, reading into personal information (texts, emails), assuming they know how their partner feels, emotionally dumping on other people or sharing information that is not appropriate, just to explain themselves or get sympathy from others.

Setting **time-related boundaries** means understanding your needs and priorities and setting aside enough time for them without over-committing. Time is a precious resource, and protecting and utilizing it is vital.

Healthy time boundaries might sound like

> ➤ "I would like to spend more time with us. Do you think we can arrange this?"
> ➤ "I'm happy to come, but I can only stay for an hour."
> ➤ "There is something I would like to discuss. When will you have time for this?"
> ➤ "I feel that your work is taking a lot of time from us. Could we talk about reprioritizing our relationship?"

Violated time boundaries look like demanding time from people, pushing in on people when they ask for space, showing up late or canceling on people because we overcommitted, contacting people when they said they wouldn't be unavailable, or forcing our partner to push their personal activities (e.g., time with friends) aside for us.

Sexual boundaries include consent, respect, agreement, and understanding the preferences of one another. With anxious attachment, we emphasize great sexual chemistry, as we often feel this is our only source to connect with our partner. A lot of anxiously attached people use sex as a way to make up for the otherwise lacking connection in their partnership, and they overstep their boundaries just to please their partner.

Healthy sexual boundaries include:

➢ Asking for consent and being flexible around timing
➢ Discussing preferences, contraception, etc.
➢ Asking the partner what pleases them and what is or isn't allowed
➢ Saying no to things that hurt you or that feels uncomfortable
➢ Not sharing sex life details without consent
➢ Not using sex to keep a partner in our life
➢ Not using sex to solve a problem in the partnership

Common sexual boundary violations are: pressure to engage in sex, unwanted sexual comments, lying about sexual health history or the use of contraception, unwanted touch or assault, sulking or punishing someone who doesn't want to have sex or using sex to manipulate.

Intellectual boundaries refer to our thoughts, ideas, and curiosity. Healthy intellectual boundaries include respect for other people's thoughts, feelings, and needs, which can be violated when we dismiss, belittle, or disrespect them. This can sound like

➢ "I know we don't agree on this, but please don't shut down because we need to figure out this problem."
➢ "I know you need time to think about this, so let me know when you're ready to discuss it."
➢ "When we talk about ..., we don't get very far. I think avoiding the conversation for now is a good idea."

➤ "I can respect that we have different opinions on this."

Learning to recognize the difference between healthy and unhealthy discourse is important. You don't need to agree or accept others' thoughts and opinions. If someone shares an inherently harmful opinion, you have every right to set a firm boundary there.

Intellectual boundary violations look like trying to force an opinion on someone, sharing unsolicited advice, or trying to influence someone or solve their problems just to control a situation. It can also look like gaslighting someone, denying the validity of their thoughts or opinions, or shaming them for thinking differently than you.

Material boundaries refer to items such as your home, car, gadgets, clothes, jewelry, etc. These boundaries are often violated when these items get damaged, destroyed, stolen, or borrowed without permission.

Material boundaries can sound like

➤ "I'm uncomfortable with anyone else driving my car."
➤ "I can't help you with money now, but I would be happy to help some other way."

103
Setting boundaries with an anxious attachment

Setting and maintaining boundaries with an anxious attachment can be difficult, for we are predisposed to believe that people will not respect them.

Personal boundaries are important to set and respect; however, **if we grow up thinking that we need to bend and adjust our ways to please others, it can be pretty challenging to learn them as adults.**

Setting boundaries is simply about communicating your needs to someone else. It isn't always easy. Not everyone will understand your needs because not everyone shares these needs. So let's review a few anxiously attached needs and how to set boundaries around them.

You need frequent reassurance from your partner:

➤ "I know you love me, but I would appreciate it if you could find a way to express it more often."

You cannot handle uncertainty in the relationship:

➤ "I would like us to talk about where we are in the relationship and where we're heading. I'm picking up on mixed signals and find them confusing."

You have bouts of anxiety every time your partner asks for time alone:

➤ "I understand that you need time for yourself, and I completely respect this. But could you check in so I know I'm important to you?"

You need your partner to discuss problems instead of shutting down:

➤ "I understand that it is difficult for you to talk about relationship problems, but let's try and find a way to resolve our issues. Let me know what you feel most comfortable with, and we'll work something out."

You need your partner to communicate clearly and consistently:

➤ "I know that you work all day and don't have time to chat, but I would appreciate it if you'd let me know that you can't talk or text back but will catch up with me later."

You get jealous of your partner looking at other people:

> "I know you love me, but you checking out other people makes me really anxious. Could you be more mindful about this when we're together?"

Always communicate your needs calmly and respectfully. Don't shame, criticize, or be demanding. **Simply state your needs and ask your partner to meet them. Also, remember that honoring your partner's boundaries is as important as asking them to respect yours.** If anxiety resurfaces, challenge your thoughts. Ask yourself if this worry, anxious thought, or fear is valid or only stems from your anxiously attached fears and insecurities. Practice self-soothing and reflecting instead of reacting.

104
Setting flexible boundaries

Be sure to set flexible boundaries and revisit them occasionally. **Anxiously attached people often start shifting towards secure attachment as soon as they become more relaxed in the relationship.** So be sure to let your partner know that your needs have changed, especially if you set boundaries they find hard to meet.

Equally, let your partner know if they aren't meeting your needs. After all, we are human and lead hectic lives filled with work-related responsibilities and other problems. Don't be afraid to remind your partner what you agreed on. Learning to speak our needs is vital for a healthy partnership.

It is important to remember emotions are not mutually exclusive. You can be both a loving and caring person and set healthy boundaries.

You can be aware of your needs and simultaneously hold space for your partner's needs. You can be both insecure and learn to trust your partner.

105
Improve your relationship communication skills

We've all heard the phrase "communication is key" probably one too many times, but for many of us, it's unclear if we go wrong. Most of us with anxious attachment likely picked up several communication strategies that we are unconscious of and that get in the way of problem-solving or getting to know our partner. Communicating effectively in a relationship means that you and your partner can have open, honest conversations about the topics important to you. It means that you can share your thoughts, feelings, or needs without any unease of being judged, shamed, or blamed. It also means that you provide each other a safe space to be understood, nurtured, and completely yourselves. In previous chapters, we discussed the communication techniques that work against us in our relationships; now let's talk about the ones that help us.

Find the right place and time to talk. With anxious attachment, we believe in the here and now. As soon as a problem arises, we want to discuss and solve it. It is understandable, as conflict activates our attachment system, and we try to get back to a regulated state as soon as possible. So we often run into difficult situations by trying to rush our partner or reacting instead of reflecting and responding. So the first step towards successful communication is to find the right time and place. As your partner, when would be a good time for them to talk or let them know you will need to discuss an issue. In the meantime, learn to sit in the discomfort of your thoughts and feelings and practice self-soothing.

Ask open-ended questions and practice active listening. Get curious about your partner's why. Take turns asking questions, and allow each other to express yourselves without interruptions.

Encourage your partner to share, even if they find it hard. Many people have been shamed or criticized for sharing emotions and have learned to hide and compartmentalize them. Letting them know they are safe will be encouraging.

Communicate your needs directly. In previous chapters, we discussed dysfunctional communication techniques and how they hinder the success of problem-solving. Try to keep these to a minimum. When you need to share something, say it calmly and directly. Don't beat around the bush; instead, say what you mean clearly and concisely. If a problem arises, share it with your partner as soon as possible. The longer you let it fester, the more difficult it will be to resolve.

Clarify the things that are unclear. Anxious attachers are often guilty of assuming instead of asking directly. So if you don't understand something, ask for clarification. Otherwise, you let your imagination get the better of you, creating wild assumptions around the most straightforward situations.

Validate your partner's thoughts and feelings. This is vital and should be done even when you disagree. Validating your partner's feelings will let them know you understand them and can sympathize with their pain. A simple "I hear you." or "I understand how painful it is for you." can go a long way.

Speak from your perspective and use 'I' statements. Speaking from your standpoint will ease the pressure, showing your partner that you aren't blaming, shaming, or criticizing them. Let them see you speak your experience, perspective, or version of the truth. Essentially, it means saying, "I feel let down." instead of "You keep letting me down."

Understand first, respond second. Making sense of what you just heard before you react is crucial to prevent conflict. Take your time and ask more questions if you need to. Work towards understanding your partner's perspective. Put yourself in their shoes. They are different from you and might see things entirely differently. Working towards seeing the situation from their perspective will help you understand them much better.

Curb your disappointment. This is tricky because it is often inevitable to get offended or disappointed by our partner's opinion. However, try to delay your reaction to disappointment to keep the discussion constructive. This will help you stay present and take in everything your partner says.

Stay regulated. Finally, work to remain regulated. If you are getting overwhelmed, step away from the conversation and take a few deep breaths, or ask your partner to continue another time.

106
Common anxious attachment triggers and their resolution

Not getting a timely response from our partner. This is one of the most common triggering events for an anxious attacher. The anxious partner sends out a message and doesn't hear from their partner for hours, often even for days. This is triggering because the anxiously attached person builds their sense of safety on the partner's presence and, in this case, their responsiveness. Having this sense of security taken away creates instability and hypervigilance, prompting them to pull closer and text more or call.

First off, we should be aware of what the text signifies. It's not the text itself or the speedy response we crave; it's a sense of safety and belonging. Knowing that our person is thinking about us and factors us into their day is why we place such importance on the speed of the response. But the truth is that we all lead busy lives and have jobs, responsibilities, and an instant answer to a text message should not be the standard. It is something that comes over time as the relationship progresses. So instead of emphasizing the issue, try and relax into the relationship, pace yourself, and regulate your nervous system. Relax your expectations for instant validation and learn to sit in the discomfort that is part of being together with someone. Notice all the little ways your partner shows love for you and work to cultivate safety within. If you feel the need, put healthy boundaries around this and let your person know that their lack of responsiveness gives you anxiety.

Our partner is not reciprocating our communication style and has a different love language. Another common issue for the anxious person is their partner expressing their love in a different or a more toned-down way. This speaks to our wounded inner child that needs a lot of reassurance and validation. Anxiously attached people can be very affectionate and usually have no problem showing their feelings for their partner. They are giving, loving, and show their hands quite plainly in love. That's why meeting someone who communicates their love less intensely can be so triggering, as we often take it for indifference.

This can be discussed, and I encourage this to be addressed at the beginning of the relationship. Share your love language and your needs with each other. Giving and receiving love is different for everyone, so talk about this openly with your partner, tell them your needs, and try to navigate your differences to find common ground. Allow each partner to be authentic in the partnership. Give room for each other to express your feelings the way and at a time you feel comfortable, and don't push it too hard. Instead, try to notice the subtle ways your partner shows up for you. Perhaps they feel uncomfortable saying 'I love you' daily, but they bring your favorite coffee to bed each morning. Or they don't take you out on fancy dates or buy you flowers, but they will always pick up your favorite chocolate when shopping.

Our partner takes longer to realize or verbalize their feelings for us. As anxiously attached, we tend to go from 0 to 100 in what feels like mere minutes when we start dating someone. It's so exciting, fresh, and promising. The honeymoon period is our preferred state of being in a relationship, with constant communication, reassurance of our partner's love, and physical intimacy. All emotions are heightened, so falling head over heels in love with the other person is much easier. It is also easier to say so. But what happens when our declaration of love is not reciprocated? That's a first blow and usually quite a big one. We immediately start questioning their intentions and our worth and start going into panic mode. Our activating strategies and protest behaviors switch on, and we become needy, clingy, and unreasonable.

There is no easy solution to this problem besides being patient and noticing the nuanced ways your partner shows up for you. Perhaps they aren't ready to declare their love for you, but they show signs of wanting to include you in their lives. You can't rush anyone to catch feelings for you, so learn to stay in the discomfort of not getting your needs met instantly. On the other hand, if you notice your partner being reluctant to show their feelings, are indifferent to you, or give off mixed signals, then have an open conversation about it and ask them where they stand.

Our partner needs more time alone than we do. This is a trigger I often come across, especially if the partner is avoidantly attached because their way of self-soothing is isolation, while the anxiously attached way is connection. This seems like a catch-22 for anxious partners, but there is no reason to worry. First, you need to understand that your partner's need for healthy space has most likely nothing to do with you. It doesn't reflect on your relationship and is unlikely to impact it negatively. Simply put, it is a basic human need to recharge and reconnect with ourselves. In fact, anxiously attached people should practice taking healthy space for themselves more often.

So when your partner asks for space or time alone, you should try to meet their needs with respect and compassion. There is no reason to get scared; if you feel triggered, practice self-soothing and getting out of the situation until you are completely calm. Go for a walk, splash cold water on your face, or take a few deep breaths. Practice empathy and try putting yourself in your partner's shoes. Opening up your perspective and supporting your partner's needs is a secure trait your relationship will benefit from. Ask them questions if needed and set up a way to meet halfway. For example, he takes the weekend to himself but checks in with you daily over the phone or keeps in touch through texts. Remember to practice calming your nervous system and try to take this time to focus on yourself and meet your needs. If this is a need that comes up frequently, you could even try to work out a routine to help set healthy expectations and curb your disappointment.

Our partner makes decisions without confirming or discussing them with us first. This can be highly triggering for those of us with anxious attachment because we can interpret it as a sign of abandonment. We often think they would have involved us in the decision-making if we were important enough for them. Black-and-white thinking is not going to help you improve the problem. If this is an ongoing issue for you, it's worth talking to your partner about it and setting healthy boundaries around making decisions involving both of you. This usually sets things right, and having the reassurance you need resolves the issue. Additionally, you must learn to be more accepting and flexible about your partner's schedule. They may need to make plans or decisions without you occasionally, which is entirely ok.

Our partner has a healthy social life and regularly goes out with friends and colleagues. Anxiously attached partners can find this threatening, as in their interpretation, it takes away from their connection with the partner. This is when their subtle manipulation tactics kick in. They may accuse the partner of infidelity, suggest they neglect, or try to get them to cut their interactions outside the relationship. Often the anxious partner tries to push on their partner's plan with their friends, organizing group activities or simply inviting themselves to their gatherings. This is frequently caused by a fear of being alone or losing the partner if they spend time outside the relationship. Anxious attachers have a tough time finding other focus points when in emotional distress. Because of this, they have a more challenging time implementing a problem-solving approach to emotional stress.

Learning to be content alone, widen your interests and activities, and have a healthy social life is the solution. And while this sounds completely normal, it can be much harder to implement when in emotional distress. So practicing self-soothing and taking yourself out of the triggering situation is a great place to start. Be kind to yourself and your partner. Understanding and normalizing that you both have different needs will take you one step closer to a secure attachment.

Jealousy caused by threats and perceived threats. This is a prevalent trigger for the anxiously attached. While jealousy is a normal human emotion that we all feel from time to time, anxious people tend to have an exaggerated reaction to threats or perceived threats to their relationship. Jealousy in a relationship can create friction and distance between the partners, negatively impacting both partners, not only the one who feels it.

According to several studies, jealousy manifests as anger and irritability in anxious-preoccupied people and is often left unexpressed. Furthermore, the anxious partner is more likely to engage in surveillance behaviors and gets hypervigilant in the face of a threat. The work here is to communicate your feelings and insecurities to your partner. While it might initially be intimidating, research shows that sharing your jealous thoughts with your partner helps build intimacy. It also helps your partner understand that even the slightest flirtatious behavior can act as a massive trigger for you. It's important to remember that your partner cannot just assume what you feel or think. Sharing your perspective might help shift your partner's by making them understand and respect your needs and boundaries better. Another proven way to reduce jealousy is physical touch. It counteracts the overpowering energy of the physical trigger and helps soothe your anxious thoughts. So when you feel the emotion coming up, try leaning in for a hug or reaching for your partner's hand. Studies show that physical contact has a proven way to reduce anxiety and build connections in relationships.

Physical distance between the partners. This is a challenging trigger, even for securely attached people. Physical distance can trigger anxiously attached people, causing them to question whether they have a real connection with their partner.

This fuels their activating strategies:

- ➢ Thinking about the partner with difficulty concentrating on other things
- ➢ Remembering only the good qualities, putting them on a pedestal
- ➢ A constant feeling of anxiety that only goes away when in contact with the partner
- ➢ Believing this is their only chance at happiness, perhaps even that they are the one

These activating strategies trigger protest behaviors – getting clingy, picking fights, going no contact – and these behaviors lead to further conflict with their partner, fueling their anxiety even more. This is a vicious cycle that can contribute to breaking down the relationship in the long run.

To avoid getting caught up in this cycle, try working out a schedule to catch up frequently during the long distance. Seeing each other in regular intervals, taking daily calls or face times, and staying in touch throughout the day via text messages can help soothe the anxiety. It can also set healthy expectations for the anxiously attached partner by not having to second-guess when their partner reaches out next. Try making in-person meet-ups special, make date nights and day trips, and focus on each other when together. When you're alone, engage in solo activities and work out a weekly routine to help soothe yourself. Pick activities that you enjoy. This will shift your focus to looking forward to and enjoying your alone time.

Our partner is trying to reinforce the boundaries that we keep ignoring. Setting and respecting boundaries in a relationship isn't a strong suit of the anxiously attached. In fact, we tend to overstep our own boundaries, let alone those of others. So every time we face a situation where our partner tries to set or reinforce a boundary, we interpret this as a way of being rejected or excluded from their lives. In these situations, we exhibit protest behaviors trying to get our partner to work for us or earn our love. We may react by pushing them away, giving them the silent treatment, getting more clingy, or simply getting angry with them.

The work here is to show more respect for your partner's needs, get curious about them, and ask why they set this boundary and what the need is behind it. Be empathetic and receptive. Show understanding of your partner's needs, and understand that they have a life outside of the relationship, work obligations, family, hobbies, etc. Try to take yourself out of the equation; your partner is likely reinforcing their boundaries to maintain a healthy relationship balance with you and not to push you away.

Never saying no, allowing the resentment to build up, resulting in a sudden outburst of anger. Both partners have needs in a relationship; ideally, these needs are met with equal effort. However, this is a one-sided game for the anxiously attached, for they learned to abandon their own needs to maintain a connection with their attachment figure. This looks like never saying no, offering to help our partner or take over their responsibilities, agreeing to things we don't want, or accommodating behavior that oversteps our boundaries. This can reach a point in the relationship where the anxious partner starts playing the giver, fixer, or caretaker. This behavior, no matter how well intended, has a way to backfire. Like all codependent behaviors, this will inevitably build resentment in the anxious partner, who feels used and overlooked in the relationship. This may erode the partnership in the long run, for the anxious partner will start feeling that their needs are unmet and thinking of the partner as selfish or unloving.

The work here is to start setting healthy self-boundaries and focusing more on your own needs. Stop glorifying unhealthy boundaries in the name of love. You don't have to give, fix or care for others to be loved. Learn to treat your partner as an equal, and let them make their own mistakes rather than solve their problems for them. Reflect on your behavior and catch yourself when you overstep your boundaries.

Setting healthy self-boundaries looks like

> "The next time I am invited to an event I don't want to attend, I will kindly decline without overexplaining myself."
> "When I share my feelings with my partner and get criticized, I shut down. I can only share anything with them if they respectfully respond."
> "From now on, I will only help others if it fits my schedule and I have the mental and physical energy to do so."
> "The next time my partner mentions a task, I will not offer my help without checking if I have the time or energy to do so."

We are criticized and cannot take it in a healthy way. Seeing ourselves through someone else's lens is difficult, even when feedback comes positively. However, learning to accept positive criticism and apply it when needed will add a lot of self-awareness and let us practice compassion and openness. That being said, not all feedback is positive, nor should we consider or apply all. Feedback is usually delivered from everyone's perspective and doesn't necessarily reflect our own opinion. So how should we take criticism without deflecting or self-shaming?

Try to take criticism sincerely. Sit with the information without deflecting or judging. Don't respond; just think about what you heard. Do you agree, do you disagree, do you agree and still think your behavior is valid or justified? Remember, it's up to you to decide what you want to do with the feedback you get. Just because someone criticizes you doesn't mean you must take it into your stride and categorize yourself as flawed. On the other hand, if it's something you are aware is impacting your life, consider taking a different approach. Also, consider the source. Does this criticism come from someone who knows you well, loves you, and understands your reasons? Sometimes, even the most well-intended criticism can be ill-informed, so filter who you let information in from.

107
How to share your attachment style with your partner?

How you and your partner relate to each other, solve problems and reconnect after conflict often comes down to your attachment style. **Letting your partner know about your attachment style will give them an insight into how you grew up, what family dynamics you experienced, and what you bring into the relationship.** Understanding who you are in a relationship will give them more clarity to connect the dots and understand why you act the way you do. Showing them who you are might help them open up about themselves and share insights into their story. In my experience, vulnerability deepens the connection between partners, so don't be afraid to show up authentically and share the bad bits too.

So here are my top tips on sharing your attachment style with your partner:

> ➤ Find the right time and space to bring up the topic.
> ➤ Stick to speaking from your perspective, sharing your experience, and giving them examples if needed.
> ➤ Talk about what an attachment style is, how it develops, and what your anxious attachment means in the context of romantic relationships.
> ➤ Share how it impacts your ability to connect, what fears you might have, and what the most important thing is for you in a romantic partnership.
> ➤ Share your needs, boundaries, and how your partner can help you meet, set or respect them.

➢ Talk about what happens when you get activated, the following protest behaviors, and how your partner can help you reconnect or de-escalate conflict.

➢ Share the ways you are working on your anxious attachment; learning more about what triggers you, self-soothing, rewiring your trigger reactions, etc.

➢ Share the great qualities anxiously attached people have

➢ Encourage your partner to ask questions.

108
Share what it feels like being anxiously attached

Acknowledging our emotions is difficult enough, let alone sharing them with our partner. It can feel vulnerable and often overwhelming, but sharing is critical in building a healthy connection. Talking about our anxiously attached feelings builds trust and harmony, so practice opening up. Your partner may experience the same situation entirely differently than you do, and unless you share your perspective, they will never really understand what you're going through. Remember, we perceive our thoughts and interpret our feelings differently based on our personalities, upbringing, and life experiences. What might be painful to you can be entirely neutral for your partner, like taking time apart, not talking daily, or not moving in together.

Sharing your anxious attachment sounds like this:

➢ "When my anxious attachment gets activated, I do things that are out of character just to get your attention, like texting you repeatedly or obsessively thinking about us and how to fix our relationship."

➢ "I need a lot of reassurance to feel comfortable in our relationship. I am working on becoming more self-assured, but in the meantime, I would appreciate you showing me more affection and reassuring me about our relationship. It would help me feel at ease."

109
Share your triggers

Help your partner understand what triggers you, so they can pay attention and avoid it. Remember, sometimes you will have to repeat yourself and express your needs over and over again. We all lead busy lives, and sometimes information just slips us by, and we don't notice it. So don't be offended if your partner forgets something; we are all human. Talking about our triggers is hard, especially as we surround them with disproportionate shame. It will be challenging to open up at first, but remember, practice makes better. Consider your partner's personality and preferred communication styles to communicate your triggers effectively. Sharing this with a secure partner will be completely different than an avoidantly attached partner. Be calm and collected, and use descriptive language. Speak in 'I' statements, as in speaking entirely from your perspective, describing your own experience to ensure your partner doesn't think you are blaming. Say, 'I feel anxious when you don't return my calls for hours' rather than, 'You never return my calls on time, and I hate that.' Have a conversation about how to resolve this, don't just assume that your partner will automatically know what to do. We are all different, so if you want your needs met, then express them clearly.

110
Tell your partner how you react when you're triggered

Even if you are an open book to your partner and communicate your needs and boundaries well, they still might not understand your reactions in every situation. Our actions and reactions are personal and based on who we are and how we learn to see ourselves and the world around us. Anxious attachment often puts a strong negative bias on things, so explaining your why is crucial to better understanding each other. It helps deepen your connection and build intimacy. Be vulnerable, courageous, and self-aware.

A few examples:

- ➤ "When you look at other women, I get angry and disappointed. I feel that you might be keeping your options open, which triggers my insecurities. That is why I shut down completely and get defensive about everything you say."
- ➤ "When you are late, even though I told you repeatedly that I find it disrespectful, I get distraught. I feel that it reflects my worth, and it makes me think that I mean nothing to you. I get so overwhelmed that I cannot verbalize my feelings, so I give you the silent treatment."
- ➤ "It makes me anxious when you pull away emotionally or physically, and I instantly think of worst-case scenarios. I am upset and feel betrayed, so I start catastrophizing and pulling back from you. But it's a cry for help; I want you to notice I'm hurting."

111
Co-healing

We are social beings and need connection with other humans on an individual and community basis. We form and maintain new connections with people throughout our lives, including friends, colleagues, school friends, neighbors, professional acquaintances, and many more. It's down to us how we nurture these relationships; however, many studies suggest that the ideal interpersonal environment is made up of more positive and nurturing connections than burdensome ones. Positive relationships help us heal, as being loved, supported, and understood by others can help us live a balanced, fulfilled life.

In a relationship context, co-healing is a fantastic practice where two people commit to support each other through their relationship, providing a safe space to heal, unlearn, change, and grow. **The process of co-healing includes actively listening, empathizing, working to change ourselves, loving our partners, being there for**

them, and letting them know they matter despite our problems or differences. We can practice co-healing with our partners in many ways, and I list the most prominent ones below.

Active listening. Stay present with your partner when they share something with you, even if it's painful to hear. Shift the focus from defending yourself or explaining your behavior to empathizing with your partner's feelings. Put yourself in their shoes and stay present. What we often need beyond a viable solution is someone who can hear, see and open up to us. So being an active listener for your partner can go a long way.

Empathizing means putting yourself in your partner's shoes working towards understanding their feelings and pain, and validating it while holding space for your own. Being able to read your partner's body language effectively will help a lot, as often we express anger while we have underlying feelings of sadness or loneliness. With anxious attachment, our first instinct when facing a problem might be to try and solve or fix it. So instead, try to stay present with your partner and show them compassion. This 'shared pain' will help you connect on a deeper level.

Willingness to change starts with sharing your needs and concerns with your partner regularly, not only when things reach a tipping point. Do you need your partner to help out more or reach out to you during the day? Let them know! Then work towards meeting each other's needs. This will signal to both partners that relationship needs are taken seriously and will allow them to lean on one another more comfortably.

Make space in your life for **love, fun, and playing**. Express your feelings for each other, and not just verbally. Touch your partner, act lovingly, meet their needs, and express how much they mean to you regularly. Make time for your favorite activities, pick up a new hobby, prepare a meal together, and have regular date nights. An integral part of love is that it isn't subject to the other's actions or reactions, so work toward unconditional love, support, and understanding, and make forgiveness a part of your lives.

112
Co-regulation

We first begin learning emotional regulation through co-regulation with our primary caregiver. They teach us how to upregulate positive and downregulate negative emotions. Children have limited abilities to soothe themselves and regulate their emotions when overwhelmed. It's the parent's job to teach them the basics and show them how to handle negative emotions like sadness, fear, anger, etc. Without learning healthy co-regulation in childhood, kids develop maladaptive coping strategies like suppressing their emotions and are more prone to outbursts of emotions and temper tantrums.

Co-regulation in relationships is when the partners help each other to regulate their emotions and reduce stress effectively. Co-regulation can happen through physical touch, holding hands, hugging, speaking soothingly, or verbal acknowledgment of distress. To effectively co-regulate with your partner, learn each other's preferred way of being heard, seen, and reassured. Often we want to be validated rather than offered a solution, so get into the habit of asking one another if you need active listening or a solution to your problem. Remember, co-regulation is a choice and cannot be forced or demanded.

113
Work to prevent getting triggered

We have a way of giving in to the stories in our heads, even when there are other facts to consider. We give into our negative mental chatter and let our imagination get the better of us. We make up stories about our partner's infidelity or their lack of affection. We use our confirmation bias to build the foundation of these stories, and nothing could steer us from this path. We go head first into a triggering situation and cannot find ways to pull ourselves out. Nothing works, not that we know our partner to be honest and faithful, not that they have shown a million ways that they are committed to us. So how do we prevent giving in to our own negative mental chatter before we are triggered?

> **Figure out your most prominent triggers.** We have dozens of triggers on average, and figuring out all would be incredibly overwhelming. Instead, try focusing on the most common ones and narrow it down to 2 to 3.

> Get to the bottom of **what comes before the reaction** and the immediate cause. This can be criticism or our partner wanting to take time out of the relationship. Pay attention to your state of mind. Is it more likely to happen when you are stressed or apart from your significant other?

> Next, **recognize the physical signs.** When triggered, we all have different physical reactions, including a racing heart, sweaty palms, or a knot in the stomach.

> Find a way to interrupt the cycle. Choose any emotional regulating technique that suits you, and make sure you bring your nervous system into a rest and digest state. Rest and digest is the automatic response that tells your body it is safe to focus on recovery and involves lowering blood pressure, breathing rate, and heart rate, as well as triggering other functions like digestion. When you achieve this state, you will be able to think more clearly, as your prefrontal cortex is activated again. **Visualizing something different can be an incredibly useful technique** to interrupt the negative thought cycle. As soon as you notice the physical signs, visualize something that can help take your mind off your immediate surroundings. This could be anything from driving your car on a long, winding road or looking around from the top of a mountain taking in the view. Deep belly breathing, shaking your arms, or splashing cold water in your face can be equally helpful to bring yourself back to regulated.

> Once calm, **get curious about the story** behind the trigger. Call yourself out on the negative thoughts. Where does it

come from? Is it true, or is it signaling a core wound in me? When did this happen to me before? At this stage, journaling can be beneficial to get more clarity.

➢ **Exchange the story** behind the intrusive thought. Don't let your imagination run away with you. Stay firmly rooted in reality. If your trigger is your partner taking time out of your relationship, then work to internalize the thought that it most likely has nothing to do with you. Try to understand their perspective better, why they need alone time, and leave some wiggle room for their way of doing things. The secret of anxious attachment healing is going through the experience and discomfort of uncertainty because it shows you your strength and gives you a 'this wasn't as bad as I thought perspective. When you come out on the other side of pain, you realize that your anxiety created most of the fear, and in reality, you are much stronger and more resilient than you think.

➢ Finally, **work to heal your core wound** connected to the trigger. Let's use the previous example of your partner needing time away from your relationship. The feeling of rejection is likely connected to an abandonment wound in your childhood, so that's where your work is. To heal a core wound, you need to identify it, then instead of denying the negative emotion it causes, allow yourself to feel it and let it pass.

114
Where we struggle and what can help

Clingy, needy behavior	Work on boosting your self-esteem and self-worth by noticing your good traits, accepting compliments, praising yourself for your achievements, and doing things that give you a sense of accomplishment.
Overanalyzing and worrying	Try mindfulness meditation and journal about the situations that have you overthinking. Try to go beyond and figure out the real reason why you worry. Question your thoughts.
Prioritizing others	Shift the focus back on yourself, ask yourself your daily needs, and work to meet them.
Problems with self-regulation and soothing	Practice self-soothing in anticipation of getting triggered, and work to solidify your self-regulation techniques.
Anxiety over the partner's need for space or time alone	Find new hobbies, widen your scope of interests, establish a support system outside of the relationship, and don't focus on one single person to have all your needs met.
People-pleasing and losing oneself in relationships	Reestablish your focal point on you, find out what the core values are in your life, and commit to a healthier balance.
Codependency	Work to meet your needs independently, learn to validate your thoughts and feelings, and reassure yourself in stressful situations

Fear of being alone	Find meaningful pastimes that help you discover your strengths and passions. Try community activities that give you a sense of belonging; book clubs, church, volunteering, group meditation, or fitness classes.
Lack of confidence	Find something that you are great at, giving you a sense of accomplishment, no matter how small. Start writing down all the small things that made you proud at the end of the day.
Oversharing	Think about the intimate details before you share them and try to determine if you share them to create closeness and understanding between you and the partner or if the situation justifies it.
Fear of rejection	Work on open communication and vulnerable sharing of thoughts and needs. Let your partner know how their behavior or response makes you feel, and don't be afraid to come across as needy.
Need for constant reassurance	Work to build trust in the relationship and have open communication about needs and boundaries.
Insecurity	Work to increase your self-esteem and find reassurance within. Have vulnerable conversations with your partner about needs and non-negotiables.
Jealousy	Have open communication about each other's needs and boundaries.

115
Ways to reconnect with your partner

Most of us get so caught up in our relationships, conflicts, and the unresolved problems we carry that we become almost desensitized to creating or letting in new context. We forget to play and enjoy our time together. With time, the entire relationship becomes one extensive daily routine where we're just one argument away from starting to grow apart. **A relationship takes commitment, consideration, and work.** Reconnecting with our partner takes some intentional effort, and here are some of the easiest ways to keep the spark in your life:

Keep dating

Nurturing intimacy may help maintain a healthy relationship dynamic going, even when you have ongoing issues. You can focus on physical or emotional intimacy or even share the different aspects of your lives. Keep getting to know each other over and over again. Getting to know your partner and learning about their dreams, plans, and aspirations provides a great new way to connect, even after years together.

Exercise together

Working out together proves beneficial for couples who need to spice up their routine a little. Having a hobby or hitting the gym together has unexpected benefits for couples. **According to research, couples report more relationship satisfaction after participating in joint exercises or physical activity.** This suggests that sharing a fitness goal, running together, or hitting the gym can enhance your romantic relationship.

When you work out together, you create a context in which your actions are coordinated. Lift weights with your partner or match your walking or running pace with theirs. These exercises result in nonverbal matching, which benefits both of you. Nonverbal matching helps people feel emotionally attuned to one another, and those who have experienced or participated in it report feeling more bonded with their partner.

Show your love

Showing our love can happen in many ways. It doesn't have to be a grand gesture, nor do we have to keep it for special occasions. Show up lovingly for your partner each day, even when you find it difficult. Listen to their needs and problems without trying to offer a solution, validate their thoughts and feelings, and stay present in your partnership. Show your appreciation, talk to them lovingly, and find meaningful ways to support each other.

Put connection over being right

A lot of anxious folks feel the need to be validated, heard, and seen all the time by their partner. And while these are all important factors in building a mutually satisfying connection, you don't always have to be right. Learn to let the small things pass, as mutual satisfaction is much more important than winning an argument, proving your partner something, or having your thoughts validated.

116
Meet your partner where they are

It isn't always easy to accept that our partner has a different understanding of relationships or problem solving than we do. They come from very different family backgrounds, had different upbringings, and encountered different experiences, making them view things differently. In my coaching sessions, I often see that this difference between two people is the cause of most of their conflicts, and they are not even aware of this. I mostly attribute this to a lack of clear communication because if we got curious about our partner's whys, perhaps we would not second guess and consequently get things wrong. So instead of assuming rather than asking, second-guessing, or judging, work to get to know your partner better. **Accept your partner as they are, with their traumas, problems, and shortcomings, and meet them where they are.** Acceptance builds trust, and trust creates connection.

117
Think of conflict as an opportunity

Conflict can be great and healthy and is almost certainly inevitable. Differences are bound to emerge when two people decide to spend their lives together, move together or be in a committed relationship. And the problem is never the differences but our inability to accept them, smooth over them, and agree to disagree. Staying connected during and repairing after a conflict is a skill we all need to learn, so here are the steps you can take to ensure you stay on the same page after a fight.

Follow these simple steps of conflict resolution.

- ➢ Don't shut down in the face of a negative comment or criticism. Your partner is human and perhaps lacks the skill set to express their needs kindly or lovingly. Instead, stay present, get curious, and take some space if needed.
- ➢ Ask questions and talk about the differences. Take turns. Don't just listen so you can respond. Instead, try to understand the other's perspective.
- ➢ Stay open to each other's needs, even if the idea is frightening or painful. Validate each other's feelings and try to find the middle path.
- ➢ Keep your activating strategies at bay. It might be difficult to resist being overwhelmed by difficult conversations, but try to set aside your negative feelings. Focus on the problem at hand, then work through the feeling of disappointment later.
- ➢ If the situation is resolved, try reinforcing the re-established connection with physical touch; a kiss, or a hug

➤ Learning to be present during conflict and keeping your activating strategies at bay is a skill that can help save your relationship and influence other parts of your life.

118
Establish a support system outside of the relationship

We should all place a greater importance on not getting our needs met by one person. Our partner cannot be our lover, best friend, psychologist, and the source of all comfort and reassurance at the same time. It is unattainable, and it puts immense pressure on the partnership, making it more prone to fail. **Start normalizing that some of our needs could be met either by us or outside the relationship.** Try building better relationships with your parents, reaching out to friends regularly, socializing with colleagues, looking for a gym buddy, or joining a social activity group. Establishing a support system outside the partnership will help reduce the pressure on your significant other and allow you to develop a more interdependent relationship.

119
Learn to be the agent of your own happiness

You don't have to give up control of your own life just because you're coupled up. This applies to anxiously attached people tenfolds. Don't make all your decisions dependent on your partner. Don't let their mood ruin yours, don't let their choices influence yours. **Learn to be more content independently, unaffected by your partner's everyday decisions.** We are autonomous adults. We don't need to parent our partners or keep a close tab on their lives to prove our worth. Naturally, big decisions should concern you and be run by you, but their choice of pastimes, friends, or calorie intake should stay their choice entirely. Anxiously attached people assume roles of fixing or saving, which are often intrusive and unnecessary. Instead of placing a laser focus on your partner's life, learn to shift it onto yours and develop your own hobbies, create and nurture your friend group and be the reason you are happy each day. Learn to be independent, and learn to focus on yourself more.

120
People-pleasing

People pleasing is a learned behavior we employ to keep love in our lives and keep the connection alive with our parent or caretaker, or significant other. People-pleasing means doing things for others at our own expense, things that are outside our reach or comfort zone, or simply not our responsibility to handle.

As it is initially an automatic response, this protective strategy begins primarily outside of our awareness. However, over time, it may become one of our strategies to protect ourselves when we feel unsafe emotionally or relationally. It makes sense to try and please the person you feel threatened by or with whom you want to build a connection. However, if it becomes how you handle almost everything over time, it may impact your happiness, physical well-being, and relationship satisfaction.

What people-pleasing looks like in a relationship context:

- ➢ You don't express your feelings if you think this will negatively impact your relationship
- ➢ You find it difficult to ask for help or accept help
- ➢ You take over the responsibilities of others even when you can hardly handle your own
- ➢ You say 'yes' even when you mean to say 'no'
- ➢ You don't express your needs or communicate your boundaries
- ➢ You are unable to make decisions on your own because you fear the outcome will negatively impact others
- ➢ You rarely consider your happiness, putting others first
- ➢ You fix other people's problems, try to save them, be their caretaker

- You assume roles in people's lives, overstepping healthy boundaries to please or save them
- You are preoccupied with what other people might think of you
- You apologize for everything
- You pretend to agree with people, even when you have a different opinion

People-pleasing can backfire in many ways. Putting all your effort into keeping others happy can deplete your resources, not to mention taking away time and energy from tackling your own goals or facing your challenges. People-pleasers often put their own life on the back burner to accommodate others. This might mean that they don't live life authentically and that they don't know themselves at all. So when it comes to voicing their own needs or problems, they run a blank, for they spend most of their time being there for others and don't know how to meet themselves.

121
How to stop being a people pleaser

People-pleasing has been ingrained in most of us, and in the long run, it may leave us feeling depleted and unhappy. So here are a few ways to turn this around and shift the focus back on yourself.

Recognize your needs and work to meet them rather than focusing all your energies on others. Working to recognize what you need to feel complete and safe within will help take the pressure off of keeping others satisfied. Make yourself a priority and recognize the fine line between giving out of love and giving to be accepted.
Set boundaries with others as well as yourself. This might be a difficult one, but learning to say 'no' will help you reprioritize your own life and set a healthy boundary with others. Internalize that it isn't selfish to set boundaries. It is merely self-protection.

Take baby steps. People-pleasing is a difficult habit to change, so if you find it hard to say 'no' or set firm boundaries, take baby steps. This can look like not volunteering to help with something or accepting help from others.

Take your time with responding. This will buy you extra time, with which you can reflect and decide. Learn not to say 'yes' to everything instantly. Take your time, and create a little distance between yourself and the request. This will help you decide and make the right choice.

Assess the request. Take your time to determine whether you have the resources to help. And most importantly, whether you want to. Remember, declining and focusing on your own life isn't selfish. In fact, the more content and fulfilled you are, the more you can contribute to others' happiness.

122
Don't get discouraged if you fall back into familiar patterns

Despite our best efforts, galling back into old habits is sometimes inevitable. The doubts, fears, and inner critic resurface because the new tracks aren't deep enough. Don't get angry, don't shame or guilt trip yourself. Instead, get curious about what made you slip up. Reassess your triggers. Once you know what is causing the slip, you can work not to let them control you when they happen. Be gentle with yourself. According to research, it takes a new habit between 21 to 66 days to form; however, a lot of factors might play into how fast you can start cultivating secure best practices. For example, a relationship with someone constantly triggering your attachment may delay your healing process.

Work to change your mentality. You can't change your life until you change your mindset. According to experts changing your mentality is one of the most effective ways to rewrite your life. It is trickier than you think because the brain is wired to protect us from what we don't know, and it's bent on keeping us the same because it is safer than the unknown. Keep moving forward, and don't forget to recognize how far you've come.

Don't get upset if triggers keep coming up. It takes time to reset your nervous system to neutral and teach your body to feel safe. Sometimes the triggering sensation will never completely go away, only ease up. It is normal for old triggers to resurface; after all, they have been part of your life for far too long. Unlearning an unconscious reaction and resetting your body's response to it is a big job and can take months. The change will be gradual and won't happen overnight. Moreover, you will probably get triggered even when you are secure. What changes with attachment work is that you learn to manage your reactions and responses better. It will always take conscious decisions and the proper skill set to soothe yourself when your core wound activates. But over time, choosing the appropriate response will become more accessible and more manageable.

123
How do you know you're healing?

Reprogramming your nervous system can be tricky, and since your reactions to an attachment trigger are unconscious, the change isn't always visible. So what are the signs that you are healing?

You are becoming more self-aware. Self-awareness is a beautiful skill that helps you lead a conscious life. It can stop you from repeating your old patterns and help you form new ones. You know you are healing when you become mindful of your habits and see your activating strategies kick in and protest behaviors play out, when you realize you could avoid an argument by taking time to reflect, when you notice that it's not your partner's reaction that sets you off but your own insecurities, when you realize that you don't have to work hard to earn love and you don't have to save or fix others to prove your worth.

You start questioning your intrusive thoughts. Another sign of healing is that you catch your insecure thoughts and question whether they are valid or come from attachment wounding. Instead of burying the feelings, you permit yourself to feel them, sit with them, and let them pass. You turn to them with curiosity and question where they come from, why you think them if they are there to protect you. Emotional clarity is immensely powerful and a sure sign of healing.

You start applying a bigger dose of reality to your life. This was a game-changer for me. You stop looking at things and people through the lens of your activating strategies. Idealizing your partner or potential partner stops being the norm, and you accept people for who they are instead of projecting a fantasy on them and getting disappointed every time they fail to meet it. You don't need to cling to your partner when they are a little distant, and you can give them time and space alone. You can look at situations clearly and recognize your part and your partner's in a conflict. You stop fantasizing about meeting the right person or stumbling across the right relationship and start consciously creating it.

124
Forgive yourself for your past mistakes

Self-forgiveness is a considerable part of the healing journey. It teaches you a useful reparenting technique, to separate who you are from the mistakes you have made. This way, you can learn from your choices and shift your patterns toward a positive direction rather than being stuck in endless cycles of self-shame or blame. Forgiving yourself also helps you to forgive others. With anxious attachment, you most likely kept repeating an unconscious survival mechanism and didn't realize you were doing anything wrong. So practice giving yourself a break from the mistakes you made in survival mode. Remember, you always did the best you could with the information and awareness you had. Learn from the mistakes, accept them, and move on.

125
Change may be slow at the beginning

There is an insecure inner child in all of us that wants to make changes happen immediately. When we start working on our attachment style, we have an idea of how that will turn out — a fantasy that it will be fast, with a perfect result and an almost instant change of habits. But it never happens as quickly as we'd like, and we're never perfect at it. Initially, change is subtle and slow for some, but there is no reason to be discouraged. Accept that attachment healing takes time and work to keep yourself motivated throughout the process. When you start, it is entirely ok to snap back into old ways, as it takes time to learn self-soothing successfully and put your new skills to work.

So how to work through the disappointment of not seeing immediate results? Give up on the outcome and instead focus on the next step in front of you. Instead, give up the fantasy and get curious about what it will feel like to be securely attached. Focus on the reality of it. Try to find happiness in the process of learning and forget quick fixes. Don't concentrate on perfection. Focus on moving forward. This will help you learn to appreciate subtle changes and shifts in your behavior and learn more about yourself than you ever thought possible.

126
Notice how far you've come

Finding success on your mental health journey dramatically contributes to your overall well-being. Seeing how far you've come since the beginning is a significant and rewarding part of the healing process. Monitoring your mental health progress can be ambiguous, and challenging to keep up with it. But it isn't impossible, and there are ways to measure the progress the same way you keep track of your career goals.

Set goals for your healing process and ensure they are specific, measurable, attainable, and time-bound. For example: 'In the next three months, I will learn to express my needs to my partner through clear and open communication.' Try prioritizing one goal at a time unless they tie in with each other, like expressing your needs and learning about them. Consider keeping a daily journal. It helps you get some intrusive thoughts out of your head and track how much you changed your behavior patterns since you began. Keeping a chart to measure your reactiveness or the intensity of your protest behaviors can also be helpful. We often don't recognize how everything changed until we step back to get a better picture. Monitoring your progress could be incredibly rewarding and encouraging. Ask your friends, family members, or therapist for feedback. They can also help hold you accountable and keep you on track with the work. Additionally, if you are seeing a therapist or health care professional, they can help you evaluate your progress against your established goals.

127
Ask your partner to check in with your progress

Research shows that couples who take a collaborative healing approach to the well-being of their relationship have a much better chance of reaching higher levels of satisfaction. There is nothing like positive feedback and encouragement from your loved ones, and co-healing will strengthen your relationship. And it doesn't matter if both of you need healing or just one. Working together towards a healthier relationship can help better understand each other's needs, bond, deepen intimacy, and build trust. It signals to your partner that they are important, valued and that you factor them into your life and decision-making. So do check in with your partner from time to time and follow up on your progress. We are not always the best judge of our progress, and we don't always see how far we've come. However, you might be surprised about what your partner picks up on regarding your habits, reactions, or behaviors. Try giving each other a kind and honest evaluation of your progress, and keep an open mind to the feedback. Putting in the work is worth it in the long run, even if you don't see an immediate result.

128
How to accept and navigate uncertainty?

First, you need to learn to accept the things you don't have any influence over. Certain things cannot be changed. Some people will disappoint you no matter what, and some situations will take much longer to advance than you might have patience for. So you must learn how to move forward and navigate uncertainty in a relationship. I realize that this is one of the most challenging concepts to grasp for the anxiously attached for someone who constantly strives for certainty and security, but there are certain things in life we just cannot influence.

So instead of outsourcing your powers and pursuing something that you cannot control, try learning to assess them better. **Learn to recognize what is worth your time and what isn't.** Learn to go a little deeper with your questions, and expect more clarity from your partner and yourself. Learn your limits in a healthy way, not in the overbearing, exhausting, 'having to do everything for everyone' way. Learn to accept people's shortcomings and their level of emotional awareness. Learn not to push hard for someone who doesn't want to do the same for you. State your needs, ask for clarity, repeat and accept change or learn to accept the lack of it.

The truth is that our developmental age, personality type, attachment style, and temperament are different from our partners, and often, no matter how hard we try to change, if they choose not to. Change is a personal choice. You cannot force somebody to change, and you cannot love them into changing for you. That's why it's vital to learn your limits, boundaries, and needs, so when it comes down to irreconcilable differences, you can make the right choice for yourself. In every partnership and healing process, there is a time when you need to acknowledge your and your partner's differences and either decide to accept them or move on in peace. The sooner you accept the fact that not everyone is going to be your partner on the journey, the sooner you will find someone who will want to be.

129
Reward yourself for all the work

It's important to reward yourself as soon as you successfully overcome a trigger reaction, solve a conflict, or self-soothe in a difficult situation. Why? **By rewarding yourself at the moment, your brain elicits positive emotions, teaching your nervous system that your efforts result in a positive reward.** By doing this continuously, your brain will start to link pleasure to accomplishing the task you set out and will work towards it easier. So reinforcing change is the key to making sure that it sticks. Without it, you might revert to old ways as they are familiar, easier, and more comfortable. Remember, our brain is wired to resist change to keep us safe. So rewarding yourself or celebrating your milestones along the anxious healing path will reinforce the change and help set in the new habit.

A reward can happen in many ways. Some reward themselves with small gifts, and some take time to do something enjoyable. Physical intimacy is a great motivator and a fantastic way to connect with your partner. Embrace your partner after successful conflict resolution, hug them, watch a movie, or have a romantic dinner together. If you associate your new wins with pleasure, it works not only to reinforce the change but to solidify the connection in the partnership.

130
Go easy on yourself

Self-deprecating comments are all too common with anxiously attached people. These have been sinking in since childhood and slip out occasionally: "I'm not lovable," "I know I'm not good enough." These comments usually circle back to a mistake we made previously, and we internalize them as a reflection on us. **We have to be careful with how we think or talk about ourselves because, repeated enough, our negative self-talk has a way of becoming our reality.** Remember, healing your anxious attachment is a challenging journey, and the one thing that will help you along the way is self-compassion. So show yourself some love for putting in all the hard work, and learn to stop labeling yourself or others.

Don't give up on yourself. As anxious attachers, we have an unhealthy amount of internalized blame that can suffocate our best efforts. If you experience a setback, take some time, and when you feel ready, start from where you left off. Don't blame yourself, and don't give up. Remember, change is likely going to take months to take effect. Knowing yourself and being aware of your traumas and triggers is half the job.

131
Don't assume the problem is always you

Often, our partner's unhealed trauma or attachment style has a significant impact on our behavior and can heighten our emotional reactivity. This behavior can trigger us more if our partner has an avoidant attachment style or a dismissive attitude. It can also be tough to process if they aren't good at expressing their feelings or solving problems or if they show their love and affection differently to us. There is nothing wrong with having differences in a relationship, but they can make it much harder for you to communicate or find a middle ground. Sometimes your partner might have difficulties opening up about their needs, so try paying attention to their body language and tone of voice. This will help you determine if they are anxious, uneasy, or impatient. Remember that their attachment style or love language might differ from yours, and this can play a massive part in how they react to things, relate to your relationship, and resolve conflicts. Don't be afraid to call your partner out on their negative behavior. Remember, sometimes it's them, not you.

132
It's not always your anxious attachment

An attachment style is only one segment of our complex personalities. Other contributing factors play into relational dynamics, including temperament, childhood traumas, mental health problems, upbringing, previous romantic relationships, cultural or sociological environments, and many more. **Blaming our anxious attachment for everything that goes wrong in the relationship is blanketing the real issue.** Try to keep an open mind and keep practicing self-awareness. Journalling is a fantastic tool to help you clear your mind, as when triggered, you might not always see the problem. However, writing it down and returning to it offers clarity and understanding.

133
Hold yourself accountable

Staying consistent in your efforts will bring you the best results, and holding yourself accountable will help you stay consistent. Accountability has multiple benefits, including fast-tracking your progress, increased confidence, and reduced anxiety levels. **When you hold yourself accountable, you learn to work on your anxious attachment in a more manageable and measurable way.** This allows you to accomplish change more efficiently and effectively than you would otherwise.

Work out a plan for your healing journey and the changes needed to become securely attached. Follow up with it, and try to stay on track. Get yourself an accountability partner to help you along the way. Ask a friend to follow up with your process, or keep a checklist or a diary to check in with yourself. Recognize when you fall back into your old patterns. Even subtle shifts in the wrong direction can hinder your progress, like habitually saying 'yes' to things you don't want to do or allowing yourself to catastrophize instead of asking your partner for clarification when you feel confused. Set both short-term and long-term goals. List what needs to change and sort them according to how much value they add to your relationship or life.

134
Don't self-isolate

Our attachment problems only come to the surface, mostly in relationships, because that's where our very first relationship dynamic gets reenacted. The one we experienced with our primary caregiver. **Therefore self-isolation and staying chronically single will not change your attachment. It will only delay the healing process.** So don't be afraid to date, open up and be vulnerable with others. On the one hand, it is a great way to practice secure relationship habits; on the other, it enables you to discover your patterns and triggers.

However rewarding, healing is complex, and the main reason for this is that it's lonely. **As anxiously attached, you are used to getting validation and reassurance from others, family, friends, and romantic partners. Still, the truth is that no one can help you with your anxious attachment healing.** And while you may get support from friends or your partner, the bulk of the work is down to you. You will have to get reacquainted with yourself, learn your patterns and triggers, go deep into your thoughts and emotions to find where you are blocking your happiness, and rewire it. And no one will be able to help you with this. You can expect certain shifts on your healing journey, including losing friends or partners and changing your relationship with family members. It's not discussed much, but losing friends as we evolve and our needs and priorities shift is a normal aspect of healing. In most cases, losing a connection with a loved one will clear space for people who are more aligned with us, who share similar values and can support us better on our journey.

135
Reinforce your new habits

Try to find a me-time activity that reinforces your new ways and relaxes you in the meantime. Finding time for yourself will be beneficial because it teaches you to appreciate yourself for who you are, and it also reinforces newly formed habits helping you maintain a healthy distance from your relationship. A space that is needed to clear your head, calm your trigger reactions and see things rationally. It might be going to yoga every week, journaling every day, listening to binaural sounds, or going for a walk to ground yourself. Part of healing your anxious attachment is to learn to rely on yourself and develop an interdependent relationship with your partner.

Conclusion

Everything great begins with a terrible first effort

Thank you for being here, opening up, and getting curious about your most painful memories and biggest fears. Trust me when I say you are already a massive step closer to creating a secure attachment in your relationship. Remember that healing comes with consistency, effort, and self-acceptance.

Keep practicing the exercises you learned in this book to continue your healing journey. Keep pausing and reflecting. Practice honest and open communication, setting boundaries, and honoring yourself without fear of judgment from others. But most importantly, love yourself the way you want others to love you.

References

Baum, Jessica (2022). Anxiously Attached Becoming More Secure in Life and Love

Becker-Phelps, Leslie. Insecure in Love: How Anxious Attachment Can Make You Feel Jealous, Needy, and Worried and What You Can Do About It

Bowlby, John (1988). A Secure Base: Parent Child Attachment and Healthy Human Development

Campbell, Debra Phd. (August 29, 2022). How To Rewire Your Brain To Have A Secure Attachment Style, Mindbodygreen, https://www.mindbodygreen.com/articles/how-to-develop-a-secure-attachment-style

Clarke, A. H. (2019). Why Do Relationship Insecurities Generate So Much Anxiety?

Chan, Annie LMFT (2019). The Attachment Theory Workbook: Powerful Tools to Promote Understanding, Increase Stability, and Build Lasting Relationships

Chu, Sienna LMHC (May 11, 2021). Inner Child Wounds: Identifying core wounds as the first step towards healing, Intuitive healing, https://www.intuitivehealingnyc.com/blog/2021/5/3/inner-child-wounds-identifying-core-wounds-as-the-first-step-towards-healing

Craig, A. D. (2003). A new view of pain as a homeostatic emotion. Trends in Neuroscience

Dispenza, Joe (2020). Breaking the Habit of Being Yourself
Firestone, Lisa, Ph. D., How Your Attachment Style Impacts Your
Relationship

Gibson, Lindsay C. (2015). Adult Children of Emotionally Immature
Parents: How to Heal from Distant, Rejecting, or Self-Involved
Parents, Harvard Health Publishing (July 6, 2020) Understanding
the stress response, https://www.health.harvard.edu/staying-
healthy/understanding-the-stress-response

Klammer, Shelley: How to Heal Core Wounds From Childhood,
Shelley Klammer Counselling,
https://www.shelleyklammer.com/post/how-to-heal-core-wounds-
from-childhood

Lawson, David PhD. (2020). Insecure Attachment: Anxious or
Avoidant in Love? How attachment styles help or hurt your
relationships. Learn to form secure emotional connections

LePera, Nicole (2021). How To Do The Work: Recognize Your
Patterns, Heal from Your Past and Create Your Self

Levine, Amir (2012). Attached. The New Science of Adult
Attachment and How It Can Help You Find - and Keep - Love

Lewis Herman, Judith. MD. Trauma and Recovery

Mars, Susannah (2015). Rewire Your Anxious Brain: How to Use the
Neuroscience of Fear to End Anxiety, Panic, and Worry

Medical News Today (2020). Why Self-Help Is Important And How
To Cultivate It

Nelson, Kate (March 15, 2023). How an Anxious Attachment Style Can Impact a Relationship, Verywell Mind, https://www.verywellmind.com/navigating-relationships-with-an-anxious-attachment-style-in-the-21st-century-5225019

Ogden, Pat PhD., Minton, Kekuni and Pain, Clare. Trauma and the Body

Poole Heller, Diane. The Power of Attachment: How to Create Deep and Lasting Intimate Relationships

Powell, Trevor J (July 30, 2008). The Mental Health Handbook

Pittman, Catherine M., PhD, Karle, Elizabeth M., MLIS (2015) Rewire Your Anxious Brain: How to Use the Neuroscience of Fear to End Anxiety, Panic, and Worry

The Attachment Project, The Superpowers of Anxious Preoccupied Attachment

The Gottman Institute, A Research Based Approach to Relationships

Van der Kolk, Bessel M.D. (2015). The Body Keeps the Score: Brain, Mind, and Body in the Healing of Trauma

Whitborne, S. K., (2012). Why Clingy Partners Cling

Zaid, Taha (2021). Anxious Attachment No More: The Exclusive Roadmap To Strive Towards Secure Attachment In Relationships

Vernon, Tony. Understanding an Anxious Attachment Style & How it Affects A Loving Relationship

Wolynn, Mark. It Didn't Start With You

Made in the USA
Las Vegas, NV
29 October 2023

79919905R00115